CW01329454

A LIFE WITH FOOD

A LIFE WITH FOOD
Peter Langan

Annotated and with a memoir by
BRIAN SEWELL
Introduction by SUSAN LANGAN

BLOOMSBURY

First published in Great Britain 1990
Bloomsbury Publishing Limited, 2 Soho Square, London W1V 5DE

Copyright © 1990 by Susan Langan and Brian Sewell

PICTURE SOURCES

David Bailey page 101
Alan Davidson page 85
Feature Flash pages 104–5
Bob Marchant page 30

All other illustrations reproduced by kind permission of
Richard Shepherd, Michael Caine and Susan Langan

A CIP catalogue record for this book
is available from the British Library

ISBN 0–7475–0220–X

10 9 8 7 6 5 4 3 2 1

Designed by Fielding Rowinski
Typeset by Bookworm Typesetting, Manchester
Printed by Butler & Tanner Limited, Frome and London

Contents

INTRODUCTION BY SUSAN LANGAN · *7*
A NOTE ON THE TEXT · *10*
A LIFE WITH FOOD · *11*
1 · CLARECASTLE · *15*
2 · CASTLEKNOCK COLLEGE · *41*
3 · FINDLATERS · *47*
4 · MY PARENTS · *49*
5 · THE EARLY YEARS · *51*
6 · ODINS · *55*
7 · LANGANS BRASSERIE · *63*
8 · SPECIAL DAYS I REMEMBER · *67*
9 · MY LOVE FOR THE GRAPE AND THE HOP · *69*
10 · AMERICA · *71*
11 · ENGLAND TODAY AND MY FAVOURITE HIDING PLACES · *73*
12 · MY FUNERAL FEAST · *79*
PETER LANGAN BY BRIAN SEWELL · *81*

Introduction

SUSAN LANGAN

It was quite difficult to persuade Peter, in the first place, that dictating his autobiographical cookbook directly to me at the typewriter was not a good idea. Past experience had shown that this non-writing method of writing led to a torrent of unsorted and unpunctuated clauses, admittedly containing much original thought, but given at increasing speed while the giver worked his way over to the door and made off for the pub, restaurant or art gallery (or anywhere), enjoining me as he departed to re-render what he had dictated – 'You know what I want to say.' On his return, some hours or perhaps some days later, he would read the typescript and reproach me for having put it into the English, rather than the Irish, style. Then he would get to work on improving my transcription.

It took a week of cunning cajolery on his part and po-faced refusal on mine for him to accept that his first full-length book was best written by him alone, labour-intensively, in longhand. He gave in with reasonably good grace, and went off to the office-supplies store to arm himself with HB pencils, preferably rubber-ended, rubbers of assorted sizes, Sellotape, scissors, staples, Tipp-Ex, small sticky-edged notepads and large quantities of the yellow, lined, foolscap pads without which he would write nothing at all.

This paraphernalia of the job in hand carefully arranged around his armchair in front of the television, he then took off for County Clare and Clarecastle, the place of his birth. He found there much changed, and much changed not at all, and the people whom he knew greeted him not as the noted restaurateur, but as the second son of Dan and Nell Langan, whose boy they remembered well and who had not been gone from them so very long. The old, home-ground magic worked, memory rose in him like Kundalini and he came back to Alphamstone, commissioned a friend to research and test recipes, and set to work.

The work went well. Peter was totally insomniac; so afraid of being unable to sleep that he often could not go to bed at all. He soon discovered that writing beguiled the hours of darkness, gave purpose to that still time when others are seeking renewal and recovery, but when he could find no rest at all. He amassed his cookery books for easy reference, collected current videos to provide the 'brain candy' he needed as background to almost any endeavour and settled down to concentrate his thinking. Refreshment was sought in the preparing of stir-fried snacks and the making of tea, in a chamber-pot-sized Portmeirion cup. The making of tea was clearly more refreshing than the drinking of it; usually only the topmost third of the liquid was consumed before the rest of it went undrinkably cold and the kettle had to be reboiled.

Manuscript accumulated, was typed up and submitted to his publisher, and but for the demands of his girlfriend – the one who lives in the sealed and corked green bottle – half of the book might have been completed by the time of the fire. As it was, a lot of manuscript was missing. I looked in the obvious places and the places where things had been moved to; I raked over the cindery rubble, and examined scraps of charred paper drifting around in the garden. There was no sign of the familiar sloping hand on lined yellow paper and I feared the whole project would be written off, consigned to the file marked 'Good idea, but never came off'.

Bloomsbury's suggestion that Peter's existing chapters should be published in conjunction with a personal memoir and commentary by Brian Sewell came as joyous news. Who better for this purpose than Brian, friend of long standing, though much tried and tested in his friendship, Peter's tutor in art appreciation and artistic merit, his guide through saleroom viewing and his adviser on what to buy, the friend who so generously lent pictures of quality on the easiest of terms, to complete the collection acquired for the opening of Odin's at 27 Devonshire Street. Brian was in at the beginning. He remained as a friend. He was witness to that peculiar occasion, the marriage of Peter and Susan.

I read Brian's memoir with the keenest interest. Much of what he recalls I was a party to also, but saw it from a different viewpoint, felt it in a different way. Through his words I both remember the man I knew, and wish I had known that man better.

A NOTE ON THE TEXT

Peter Langan's original manuscript is reproduced in this book exactly as he wrote it. No editorial alterations have been made, because Peter himself could neither be consulted nor give his authorization to any changes.

Peter's text, which appears on pages 11 to 82, has been annotated by Brian Sewell, whose notes are printed in *italics*.

A Life with Food

PETER LANGAN

A Life with Food intends to be a cookbook with memories from childhood, the food I ate then and what I have been eating and cooking in the three decades since.

It is to be a book of recipes interspersed with tales of triumphs and disaster. Some may remember that when I was cooking at Odins it was said to have some of the best food in London.

The darling of the Demstroids is as committed to his job as any of his more seriously treated contemporaries. My life has been varied. I have worked for a Dublin wine importer, been a petrol pump attendant, a clerk, a part time private detective, a salesman, and now, a restaurateur. I have not felt like telling the story of how Odins survived its financial crisis of 1966 until now.†

†*Odin's was all but bankrupt when Peter took control in 1966, and was urgently in need of more money than the business could immediately generate. The source of these extra funds was his occasional work as a 'tail' for a man whom he supposed to be a private detective; he gives details on p. 55 et seq.*

There is nothing conventional about me. People have told me that I am kind, vindictive, but not ruthless. I am relentless in my pursuit of what I call my expression of ambition, that is, the next restaurant, seating three hundred and fifty, in Los Angeles, to be opened in February 1988.

I have written for several national newspapers, magazines and even The Los Angeles Times, who thought my copy one third libel, the rest fine.‡

‡Peter was in great demand as a writer, both with serious publishers, who wanted cookery books from him, and with the editors of newspapers and magazines, who asked for reviews of books and restaurants, comments on racing and the art market, fragments of gossip and autobiography, and observations on almost any subject on which he might choose to express a robust or outrageous view (for such articles they were often prepared to pay at the rate of £1 for each word – this at a time when I was lucky to get £30 for a thousand). The most serious projects were never realised. When David Hockney had completed his illustrations to Grimm's Fairy Tales *in 1969 it was agreed that Peter should write his recipes and that David should illustrate them, in the most sumptuous, expensive and useless cookery book ever printed, far too valuable as a work of art to put at risk in the kitchen, but Peter could never find the time, the energy or the concentration, and though the idea remained alive for some years, no work was ever done. Ten years later, in 1980, it was suggested that he might write twelve monthly articles on French provincial cooking for* The Sunday Times Magazine; *a map of France was arbitrarily divided into twelve parts in the hope that each might have a reasonably distinguished and distinguishable cuisine, and Peter was to be dispatched with a driver and photographer on as many journeys as might prove necessary. His initial enthusiasm degenerated into panic when he realised how much work and time were involved, and he asked me to collaborate; I was to cover those parts of France that I know fairly well – Burgundy, Alsace, Lorraine, the Vosges, Savoy, Puy de Dôme and the valley of the Loire – collect menus, recipes and addresses, and make simple notes that he could use as material for comments in his own style; under no circumstances was anyone at* The Sunday Times *to know of this ruse, and he would pay me whatever they paid him, for it would make the series possible. In the end the project died because, as with the Hockney book, Peter simply could not make himself begin work on it.*

David Hockney: The Enchantress with the Baby Rapunzel, *1969. Hockney began work on his illustrations to* Grimm's Fairy Tales *in March 1969 and relinquished painting for the rest of the year. This early pull is inscribed 'almost final proof, for Peter, from David, 1969'.*

His short articles were always written just before their deadlines, often in the early hours of the morning for delivery that day. He wrote laboriously in a childish sloping longhand, wide spaced on alternate lines of the lined yellow paper that played such a ritual element for him – he was at ease on no other; his manuscripts were not always legible, and his grammar, spelling and punctuation were so poor that editors felt justified in rewriting many of his articles, extending or reducing them, for Peter had no sense of the commissioned length – this enraged him, and he swore never to write for such editors again, feeling that when his errors had been corrected or his text reduced, some virtue had been lost.

The best cookwriters since the war have been women with, of course, the odd exception.

I don't believe in Maginot Line cook-books written by famous chefs. They seem to be of use only to other great chefs with access to ingredients of the most exotic and expensive kind, in fact if you don't live near Harrods Food Hall they are of little use, no matter how much money you have!

My philosophy on cooking is "keep it simple. Then it stays fresh and beautiful".

I am known as the horizontal restaurateur, bibulous, and a man of excess. In nearly a quarter of a century, no business that I have owned has ever closed down or been sold, which not too many of my contemporaries from the early sixties can match.

What the hell – there's no sense in being a success if you don't enjoy it.

CHAPTER 1

Clarecastle

MY LOST VILLAGE

The long journey home took me thirty four years.† I left the village when I was twelve. Behind me, unknowingly, was the only identification within a community I've ever felt. When people ask me "Where are you from?" – the answer is always Clarecastle, County Clare.

†*The purpose of this journey, made in June 1988, was research for Peter's autobiography. He felt that he had been so long away from home that, although very brief visits to Ireland had occasionally interrupted what he perceived as permanent self-exile, only a long nostalgic exploration of his birthplace and his childhood haunts could revive recollections essential to the book.*

I did not know it at the time, but the moment the gates of Castleknock College in Dublin loomed before me, my childhood was over. I was to spend the next years of my life in "The House of Shaws" with remissions called holidays.

That long journey home took four hours from my house in Suffolk to the edge of the village.

I wasn't sure I was looking forward to looking back, but those four hours were long enough for me to remember the only time in most of our lives when the happiness of innocence unrecognised was the natural order of life.

THE VILLAGE AS IT WAS

My first memory is climbing into the maid's bed. Her name was Nancy. I hope it was a dream because I didn't like the old bat, but then along came Molly MacNamara who was to stay with the family until I left for England.

The West of Ireland, outside the main towns, had not changed radically for twenty years, so in 1945, it was still poverty stricken. The village was poor but children were not aware of it; my family were better off – I knew this because we had comics and two cars. My Father, Dan, ran Texaco in the southern part of the country. My Mother, Nell, was the daughter from the most popular public house in the village.

Ours was a close community. Ennis, the County town, was two miles and a million worlds away. If you are a Clarecastle man, your colours are black and white – The Magpies – and you are superior to everyone else anyway.

It makes me laugh when I see the stoves in the old Welsh miner's houses and pensioners complaining how they used to have to black them – many in our village had no stoves at all. The Hegartys lived opposite the National School in what amounted to a glorified galvanised shed. It consisted of the kitchen, the bedroom and a garret which you had to get to by a ladder. They were a family of six.

In the three-room school opposite, Mrs Doyle, Tom and Mrs Hanley educated children from five to fourteen years of age. I was educated here and went to the prison of boarding school in Dublin later.

We all went to school barefoot, during warm weather. I was not aware that the reason was to save the Government issuing voucher boots for the winter months. Everyone brought their own lunch – a sandwich was about it. We provided our own heating by scavenging the fields for fallen

Peter Langan 1969–1984 as portrayed by David Hockney and Patrick Procktor.

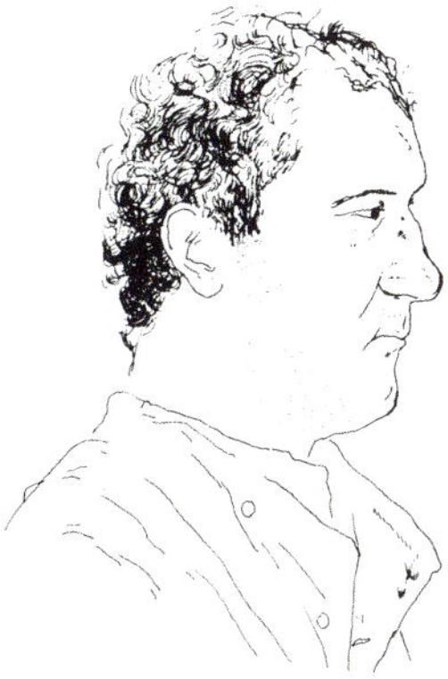
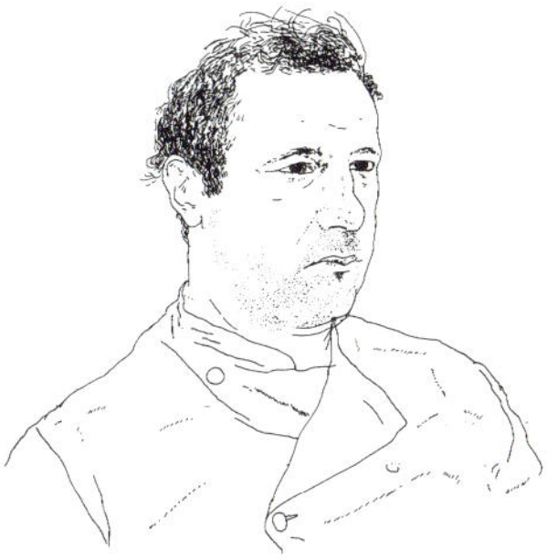
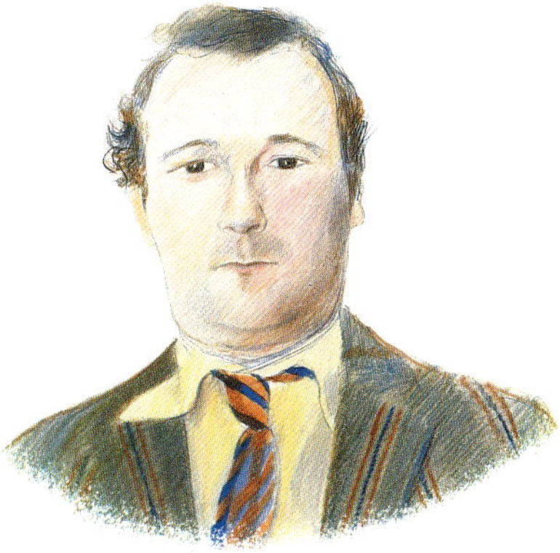
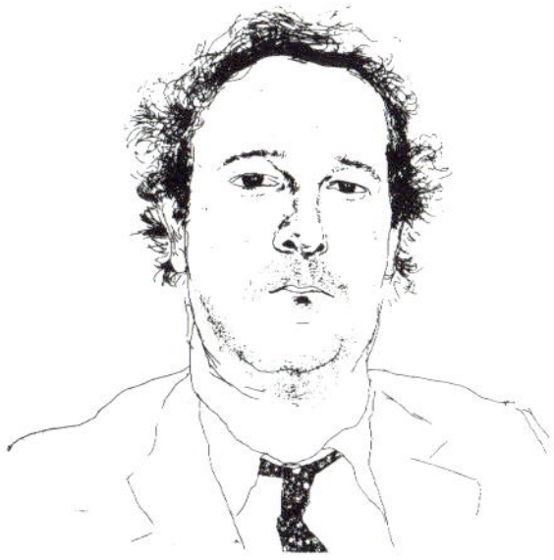
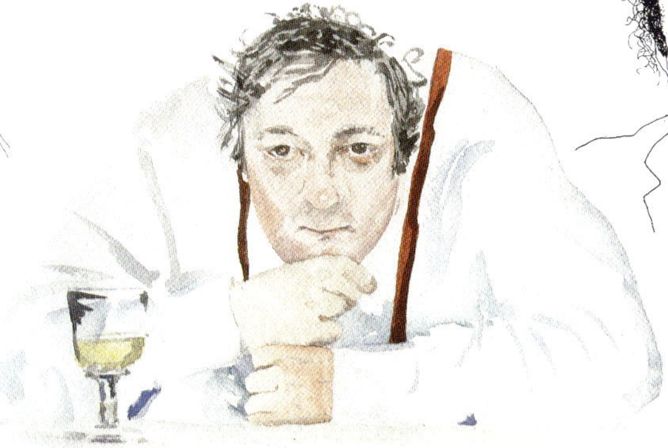
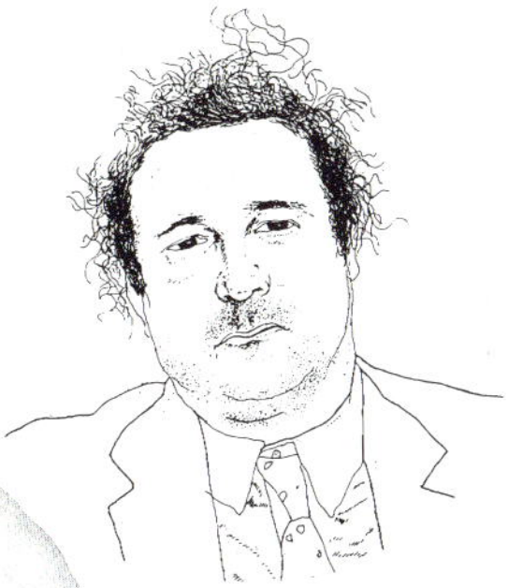
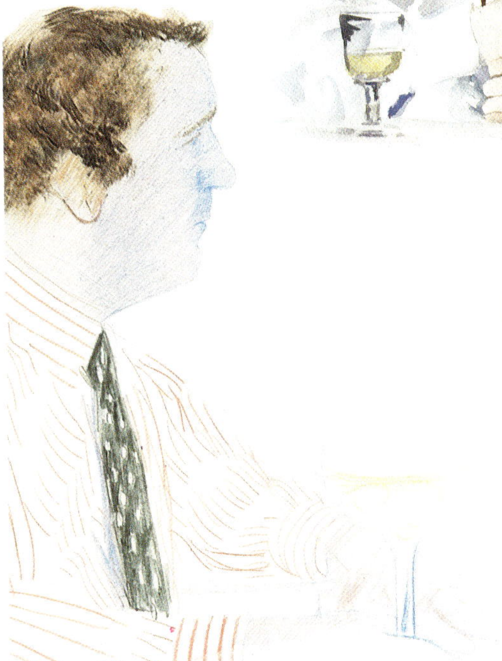
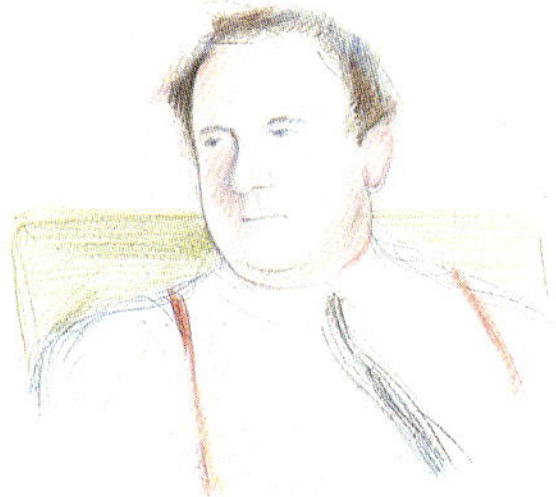
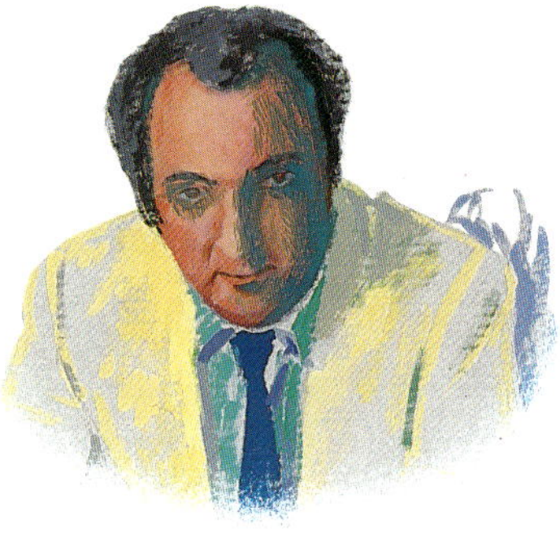

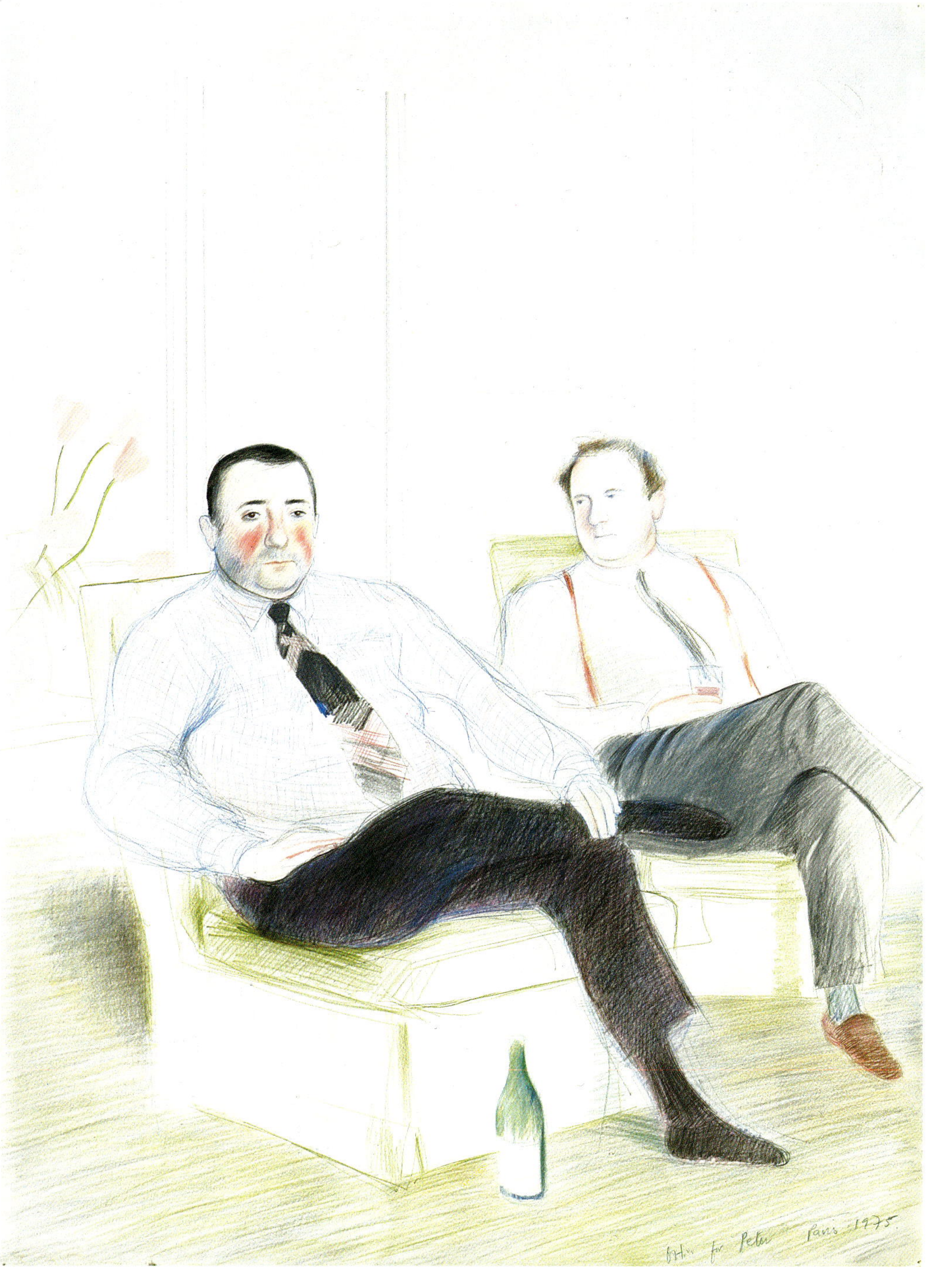
for Peter Paris 1975.

wood. We made our own fires every day. Nowadays parents complain about the number of children in a class; we were three classes in one room.

The population of the village itself was about two hundred and fifty. There was one man I hated, a Sergeant Long, who threatened me by saying I should be sent to the "back of Shaws" – I was shooting a bird with my pellet gun. I missed but Nobby Clark caught the pellet in the arse. The "back of Shaws", a sausage factory, was a euphemism for Limerick Gaol. We lost a few from the village to the gaol for dynamiting the salmon.

I had two heroes – The Conjuror, Moloney, who played hurling for the village and Terry Scanlon, who was mostly unemployed and took it out on the police. One day he took on all the Gordai and caught the pompous Sgt Long with a knockout upper-cut which meant the paddy wagon for Terry and the ambulance for Long. The joke was, who would be out first?

Just after the war, spuds and gravy and home-made bread were the mainstay diet for the unskilled, often unemployed worker, and his family, so ours was a village of emigration to England and to Australia. You left school and you left Ireland.

I was the richest boy in the village in the late forties. I looked like an angel with white curly hair, no-one even noticed how often I was hanging round my Grandmother's till. We were better off than most children and my friends, Pat Hegarty, Michael Murphy and Joe Collins, assumed I had hefty pocket money – I'm afraid it all came from my Grandmother's till.

I had been stealing for some years, for some reason we were taught that it was a mortal sin to steal a penny from a poor man, and the theft of a pound from a rich man made Hell a certainty. When you make your confirmation in the Catholic Church, you have to be in a state of grace – free of sin, or you are a sure thing for the big bonfire in the sky. I, at that time, believed in God, but I'd got used to the cash and was afraid the priest would shop me, so I was confirmed by the Bishop, thinking to myself, at least it was a Most Reverend that did me in.

David Hockney: Peter and his French Wine Merchant, *Paris 1975. Peter met Jean-Marc Moussis in Paris in the summer of 1975; their negotiations almost ruined Peter and put Odin's in jeopardy.*

Death was something that happened when you were very old, but one of the Hegartys, Joan, died in Ennis Hospital after a long illness aged about eight. The first death in my family was my Grandmother. Funerals are big in Ireland; hers was huge. The whole village shut down. She was the most benign person I have ever known.

Until then wakes meant filling stone jars with porter, sending out whiskey and everyone getting plastered. Now I know that, for some at least, it created a barrier that kept the reality of sorrow at bay – for a while.

We used to go to Clahan every Sunday. There were rock pools to swim in and smaller ones to catch crabs and shrimps. We always stopped for lobsters and crab at Liscannor on the way home. Going out in a coracle to the pots was like floating against the waves. You are at home with the sea, separated only by bowed wood and tarred canvas. I later discovered that none of the O'Donnells could swim. I asked of this fishing family, why? "Well," he said with a grin in his eye, "that way you make sure you don't fall in".

We went for our annual holidays to Kilkee where we stayed at Ma Ryan's house. She was my Grandmother's sister. She owned The Glentworth Hotel in Limerick, had one son and two daughters. The plain one, Phyllis (I'm being polite) did relieve the boredom of these holidays one night. A burglar broke in and entered her room – a mistake. She was standing on the bed with a po' full of pee which she dumped on the poor unfortunate. He was hauled off by the police, half drowned and in a state of severe shock. The story went round Kilkee that Ireland had no need of an army as long as she had Phyllis Ryan as a secret weapon. The Glentworth Hotel in Limerick dished up food that could turn a glutton into an anorexic overnight.

My Mother, Nell, was good in the kitchen and cooked all the dishes I have listed and many more. There are fifty dishes from my first twelve years. My memory is full of flavours, tastes and dreams. My Mother gave us the dishes, not the recipes. The recipes in this book are my own, except those I have plagiarised from other volumes. Rest assured, I have only stolen from the best.

THE VILLAGE AS IT IS

If you never left Clarecastle and lived there for the last thirty years, you might not have noticed the gradual but complete change. It is now a prosperous village.

Shannon airport, then an International stop-over for planes to America, would have become extinct except for one man – Brendan O'Regan – who turned it into an International Trading Centre that provides work for all the surrounding villages and towns. It even has a town centre of its own now.

The village itself, is still a strong community. The narrow roads have widened, the Church has been re-built by those who did not leave. Some of the old families still thrive – Peggy Power, who has had eleven children, still works every day in her pub and Kitty Navin is the other matriarch of the village. They will never give up. Kitty's husband, Pat, died some years ago. He had a cruel, religious maniac, alcoholic mother, who used to lock him out at night when he was a youngster if he was late home. As a result, his health ran down and he caught T.B. from which he never fully recovered. He was a kind, talented man. Pat taught himself taxidermy, was an excellent shot and painted his father and mother with great love, the only emotion he was ever capable of.

Christopher Collins (a tearaway as a child), and his friends have made certain that it will never lose its identity, even though it is now joined to Ennis by newly built houses. He has a highly successful jewellery business in Ennis and is now helping to build a new village hall in Clarecastle, helped by the Slatterys and other families.

John Hanley runs the National School. It has a dozen teachers instead of the six in his father's day. I had come back to find my roots and I did, for a short time anyway.

I had come home and was not a visiting fireman. The old men knew who I was because I look like my father. Terry Scanlon and the Conjuror Moloney, are old men now and didn't go to the Hurling Final on Sunday. We were playing Feakle and we won, of course. The game has changed, we were separated from the players by a high wire fence. In the old days, we used to have a good old riot and the match was stopped on the odd occasion.

It was at the celebrations afterwards, that I knew I was living a dream. There could be no stepping back into the past except for a short time, not

David Hockney: Peter Langan, *1969. Peter is in the small, cramped, airless kitchen of the original Odin's, wearing the stained bum-freezer uniform in which he terrorised his customers upstairs. All the equipment was of conventional domestic kind, much bashed and dented.*

now, not yet and probably never.

   Peggy, Ada, Kitty and Christy had brought me back feeling I did not realise still existed in me. My family grave is taken care of by Peggy. I am an atheist, but I was not out of place in my Irish village.

   I passed through Clarecastle on my way to Shannon Airport. My Grandmother's corner house pub, now called The Coach House, looked shabby and neglected. The rest of the village was fine. The Langan Callinan† era has passed. There were to be no goodbyes, somehow we all knew that on Sunday night. In the last few days, my time to visit had come, now it had gone. Odd though, that by a pure accident I should go there on County Final weekend and that we had won.

†*Callinan was the family name of Peter's mother.*

THE COOKING

Clarecastle Eggs
Callinan's Roast Duck
Bacon and Cabbage with Parsley Sauce
Terry Scanlon's Calves Liver
Traditional Irish Spiced Beef
Irish Stew for Auberge Père Bise
Irish Fisherman's Mussel Stew
Simple Potato Cake
Colcannon Potato
Nell Langan's Souffle Omelette
Fish and Vegetarian Omelettes
Tipsy Cake
Banana Souffle
Fay's Floating Islands

THE FIRST TWELVE YEARS

These are some of the dishes from my childhood. The old saying that "You are what you always were" is probably true when it comes to eating habits. We lived in a river village nineteen miles from the sea.

One thought about that old saying – it's a load of bull. I still eat that kind of food, but it reminds me of the priest and the benevolent, rich, randy promiscuous parishioner whom he was always trying to reform. He asked him what his favourite meal was. The priest replied with his ideal breakfast, luncheon and dinner.

He sent his friend to his house near St Tropez, full of servants etc. He was given the same breakfast, luncheon and dinner every day for a week. He returned to England and went to thank his friend for such a wonderful holiday, but said, "By the end of the week, I was rather tired of the same wonderful dishes". "Well now you understand why I get tired of the same beautiful women".

This book will cross continents, change ideas, have dinner in strange situations, meet people who would not be invited to Buckingham Palace and people who have been, but most of all, it will be about food.

Here are thirteen dishes that were regular treats as a child. I have made some more exotic than they were.

CLARECASTLE EGGS
for four

6 eggs
3 tomatoes
2 tablespoons mayonnaise (approx.)
English mustard or Dijon – to taste
2-3 anchovy fillets or smoked salmon pieces
lettuce heart leaves and watercress
2 spring onions

This is simple, quick, easy and cheap. Boil the eggs hard, let them cool. Halve. Scoop out the yolks into a bowl – mix in finely chopped anchovies, mayonnaise and mustard. Get a good smooth thick filling.

Cut the bottom off the six whites and pile the mixture back into each half egg.

Put the lettuce leaves, watercress and tomatoes into a bowl. Mix in the vinaigrette you like, then pile this mélange on to four plates. Place 3 stuffed eggs on each plate and sprinkle on the chopped spring onions.

The reason I have used six eggs instead of four is modern eggs are all white and no yolk. If you have good eggs it will taste far better, and four will do.

ROASTING IN GENERAL
but Callinan's Roast Duck in particular.

This was my grandmother's only contribution to good eating. A saint she was, and in the village, to people like Peggy Power and Terry Scanlon, she still is, but a great cook she was not.

for four

one 4½lb fresh duck (cleaned weight)
4 large onions
7 large potatoes
butter
apple or dried apricot sauce

The classic error the inexperienced cook makes is to overstuff the bird to be cooked, often with raw forcemeat. This applies particularly to birds like turkey. It forms a brick in the cavity, and then they wonder why the poor bugger tastes like cardboard. If a raw forcemeat is used the cavity should never be more than half full or you are inviting Salmonella poisoning. I have heard even the great Jane Grigson say cook your stuffing separately; frankly this is balls, and not stuffing at all.

I digress, back to the duck. The point of any stuffing is that it should absorb the juices of the bird. I generally use pre-cooked or dry breadcrumbs with herbs, a knob of butter, chopped raw onion and an egg for a little binding. Simple, but superb.

Callinan's stuffing for duck is easy. Boil the potatoes and mash them. Sauté the chopped onions in butter until cooked, but not coloured. Then blend, mince, or chop to a pulp. Add the mashed potato until you have a suitably solid, but wet mixture. You now season with salt and pepper. The onions are sweet so you will have to add more salt than you think. Season heavily with pepper – freshly ground if possible; it is ready when it suits your own taste.

I don't waste time tying the bird up with string – I cut the bit of neck that's left on the bird off, flap over the skin and skewer it to the carcass underneath. Use two skewers if you are not happy – at the other end, break the pope's nose so that it bends backwards. Load the bird with the stuffing three quarters full, (it is already cooked). Proceed as before, pulling the flappy skin over the pope and securing with as many skewers as you feel will parcel the duck up. It will look odd, don't worry, you remove the skewers just before serving. Roast the duck as you normally do. I start off at Gas Mark 6 for 30 minutes, and then reduce to Mark 4 for the next hour and five to ten mintues or so. Some cooks like to do it the other way round and every oven is different no matter what the lying manufacturers say. Professional cooks often turn the bird on it's breast for a while. Don't – it's a waste of time. There is nothing underneath the bird, so put it in a roasting pan where it is not tight against the sides. That way the whole bird will be crisp.

The sauces can be anything you feel like. The dried apricots should be soaked, then boiled and puréed, season and add a dash of brandy.

If you reduce the amount of potato and onion mix and add a tin of drained tinned chestnuts – it's an easy cheat for a chestnut stuffing.†

†*I quite see why Peter recommends the 'easy cheat' of tinned chestnuts – it suggests that he never learned the skill of skinning them. In the week before its first Christmas I spent a day with him in the larger Odin's, helping with the first stage in the production of a vast quantity of chestnut stuffing – removing the skins; we tried soaking them in hot water, but only scalded our fingertips when we attempted to split the skins and pull them back; we tried boiling them in their skins and letting them cool, but this was even worse, for the bitter brown inner membrane tainted the flesh; we tried soaking them in cold water, but this hardly affected them at all. We found the chestnuts inconsistent in their response to all these treatments, a few encouraging notions of success, but all others obstinately requiring an alternative attack. Tinned chestnuts save much time, frustration and pain.*

I have been long-winded about this simple roast because the principles apply to so many dishes. A cook needs basic information without prolonged instruction, then you let your imagination fire.

Soon after Peter became involved with Odin's he expanded the choice of food considerably. This menu dates from his early days at the restaurant.

ODINS

26 DEVONSHIRE ST. LONDON W.1.   WEL 7296

HORS D'OEUVRES

Prawn Cocktail 3/6
Scotch Smoked Salmon 6/6
ODIN'S HORS D'OEUVRES 4/6
Paté Maison 3/6
Avocado Vinaigrette 3/9
Avocado with Prawns 4/9
Escargots du Chef 4/9
Egg Mayonnaise 2/9

SOUP

Cream of Onion 2/-
Clear Vegetable 2/-

OMELETTES

Mushroom 3/9
Aux Fines Herbes 3/9
Ham 4/3
Asparagus 4/3
Cheese 3/9
ODIN'S chicken liver/mushroom 4/9

MAIN DISHES

Fried Scampi/Tartare 7/9
SCAMPI PROVENCAL 8/6
Scampi au Vin Blanc 8/5
Fillet of Plaice Richlieu 4/9
Fillet of Plaice Meuniere 4/9
Entrecote Steak au Poivre 21/-
Veal Escallope Garni 7/6
Wienerschnitzel 8/6
ODIN'S MIXED GRILL 10/6
Calve's Liver Piemontaise 5/9
Grilled Calve's Liver, Mushrooms, Tomatoes 6/3
Grilled Pork Chop   "   "   6/5
Grilled Entrecote   "   "   7/6
GRILLED PORK CHOP, DIABLÉ 7/9
1/2 Roast Poussin, Bacon, Chipolata 7/6
Calves Sweetbreads Fried 6/6
Calves Sweetbreads in White Wine 7/3

VEGETABLES

Petits Pois 1/-
Haricots Verts 1/-
Buttered Cauliflower 1/-
Pommes Frits 1/-
Mashed Potatoes 1/-
Green Salad 1/-
Salade Mimosa 1/6

DESSERT

Cream Caramel 1/6
Coupe Jacques 1/6
Cassata 1/6
Pear Belle Heléne 1/6
& Cheese 1/6

COFFEE 10d
PASTRIES 1/6

***
BRING BOTTLE   NO CORKAGE

BOILED BACON AND CABBAGE WITH PARSLEY SAUCE
for 4-6

3-4lbs corner of gammon
1 head of cabbage
1 pint of parsley sauce

There are two dishes that are Irish to the core – this is one of them.

If it is smoked gammon, soak it overnight in water, then put it into fresh cold water and bring it to the boil. Remove, skim and simmer for 30 minutes per lb.

The old Irish way is to add the cut up cabbage to the pot for half an hour toward the end. I do not like this. I prefer to boil the cabbage separately for 3-5 minutes. It is a crisp foil to the slowly cooked bacon.

The parsley sauce is simple. Melt 1oz of butter, add 1oz of flour and cook until the flour is well blended. Add ½ pint of the cooking liquid slowly to begin with then the ½ pint of milk, stir, bring to the boil and simmer. Add a bunch of freshly chopped parsley – do not cook it in as most idiot restaurants do.

The bacon, crisp cabbage, and fresh parsley sauce could be the country's greatest dish. Serve it with floury boiled potatoes in their skins.

TERRY SCANLON'S CALVES' LIVER
for two

Two slices calves liver (heavily peppered)
1 heaped teaspoon brown French mustard
4 tablespoons of port
1 tablespoon water
1 tablespoon mint
1 tablespoon parsley
a good knob of butter

Method:
Heat the fry pan, the butter should bubble when it hits the pan. Cook the liver quickly on either side – remove and keep warm. First put in the mustard, then add the port and water to the pan. It will sizzle. Reduce to two tablespoons of pan juices, just enough to coat each slice of liver, this only takes seconds. Throw in herbs and stir. Pour over liver and serve.

This is a great reviver. Serve with an Irish potato cake, a light salad and a fine burgundy.

TRADITIONAL IRISH SPICED BEEF

This is for the dedicated cook who needs to start it two to three weeks in advance. It is for any special occasion from November to the end of April – it's a winter dish.

14lbs salt beef (silverside)
½oz saltpetre
1lb salt
10ozs demerara sugar
¼lb ground allspice
14 cloves
6 onions
1lb carrots
12 dried bay leaves

Rub the sugar and allspice well into the beef, leave for 12 hours, then rub in the salt and saltpetre. Leave for approx. 12 hours. Continue to baste well for 18 days in a cool place or the bottom of the fridge, if large. Cover with cold water adding the cloves, onions, carrots and bay leaves, bring to the boil, then simmer for 30 minutes per lb. It is ready but do not cut it for 10 minutes after removing from the pot. For a less spicy result baste for 10 days. If a smaller joint is required cut down the marinade and cooking time proportionately.

Serve hot or cold with boiled potatoes, cabbage and carrots, or a salad.

IRISH STEW FOR AUBERGE PERE BISE†

†*Père Bise was a famous chef and hotelier in Talloires, on Lake Annecy, whom Peter greatly respected.*

There is no such thing as The Classic Irish Stew. It was originally layers of onions, carrots, potatoes and mutton neck chops, seasoned and simmered for a couple of hours and then served. Barley is a traditional addition, but I hate barley.

However if you have enough money to buy this overpriced volume, you can afford the Langan double-cook version, said by Charlene Bise of Auberge Père Bise at Talloires, to be one of the best casseroles she had ever devoured.

The trouble with most casserole-type dishes is that by the time the gravy has taken on the flavour of the meat, the meat itself has about as much texture and flavour as the shredded pages of the *Star* newspaper.

I always cook this when there are baby carrots and English new potatoes in season, as they are an added bonus. The ingredients are divided in Part 1 and Part 2.

serves 6-8

Part 1
¼lb smoked bacon
5lbs mutton neck chops
8 medium sized carrots
8 medium sized onions
8 good sized potatoes (peeled)
1 bunch parsley
6 bay leaves – dried
2 pints of water or enough to cover ingredients
salt and pepper (be careful here)

Part 2
2 best ends of lamb
¼lb smoked bacon
12 small new potatoes
12 small new carrots
1lb runner beans (sliced) OR
1lb mange tout
2 tablespoons chopped parsley
2 tablespoons chopped chives

NOTE: this recipe can be cut in half, but remove the eye of half of the neck chops for Part 2.

Get your butcher to remove the underside bone from the best end, trim off the line of gristle that runs along the outside edge of the rack and cut away all the fat above the eye of the meat, individualising each chop, as he would for a crown roast. Nick with the point of a knife between the bones to stop contraction.

The whole point is the butcher does all the work, all you are doing is throwing away the first meat and some of the carrots from which all the flavor has been extracted. It sounds long winded but it is extremely simple.

Part 1

Cut the carrots and onions into quarters. Cut away the excess fat from the chops. Bung all the ingredients, potatoes on top, into the pot, with water or light stock. The liquid should just cover the ingredients. Bring to the boil, then simmer. After 1½ hours check the seasoning. The bacon in this recipe will make it a little saltier than the normal method. Go on cooking for another hour, ladle off excess fat from time to time, easily done by removing the pot from the heat for a moment or two.

After 2½ hours, remove from the heat, separate the liquid, let it stand so any grease can be ladled off the top. Discard the meats. Mash by hand the potatoes and carrots, blend the onions and add this to the other purée. To this, add the liquid (which will have bits of potato in it) until you have a souplike consistency. Season to taste. You now have the liquor for the new meat.

Peter and Michael Caine, photographed by Bob Marchant.

Part 2
The new potatoes, young carrots and the greens are cooked al dente, separately, to maintain their individual texture then put them in a sieve. Run cold water through to stop the cooking. Peel the potatoes. Keep them all in a bowl on one side to be added to the final stew.

Put the raw rack of lamb, ¼lb of bacon and any meat from the neck chops you may have into the soupy liquor. Bring to the boil and gently simmer for about an hour, or until tender. Two minutes before serving add the vegetables. Throw the chopped chives and parsley into the stew when serving. Carve the chops through and spoon the soupy liquor and vetables beside them.

I admit this is one of those recipes you study before embarkation, but it's easy enough when you get down to it.

IRISH FISHERMAN'S MUSSEL STEW

In Clare when I was a child the meal known as dinner was often the main meal of the day and was in fact eaten at lunch-time. In the evening you had supper, or if you were not of working age, it was called tea. This dish only used water. The French call their version Moules Marinières.

It can be foul, because restaurants often use poor wine to make it, and then the Frogs thicken it. This is the Irish version.

1 gallon mussels
1oz butter
4 largeonions (finely chopped)
3 tablespoons fresh chopped parsley
1 pint of white wine or cider
1 pint of water
1 teaspoon thyme
4 bay leaves
1lb small new potatoes
4 heads of lettuce OR *suitable amount of spinach*
1lb carrots (small new) or cut into strips and any other vegetable on hand
salt & pepper to taste

Cleaning:
Scrub the mussels pulling off the beard (the scraggy bit that hangs off the side). Move one shell across the other diagonally, using thumb and middle finger. They may be full of mud, if so they will snap easily. If they are open and don't shut when tapped discard them. The buggers are dead.

Method:
Sauté the onions in the butter until transparent. Add the wine, water, thyme and bay leaves. Boil until the mixture is reduced by nearly half. If it is poor wine, it will have lost its vicious flavour. The potatoes and carrots to be cooked separately and kept apart. Peel the potatoes.

Pour the mussels into the boiling stock, cover. Bring back to the boil, remove them from the pan, leaving the juices. Place the mussels in a large tureen or big old-fashioned soup plates. Put cooked vegetable and spinach into the saucepan juices. Season to taste cook for 1 minute then strain off the juice onto the mussels now covered with fresh chopped parsley. Serve the vegetable on a separate platter. You can use more vegetables if you like, it makes more of a meal of it. You need no main dish after this.

Most of this dish can be prepared in advance so that you only need 5 minutes cooking the mussels. Organisation is the name of the game. There is nothing better than a tureen of fish and a platter of vegetable cooked in the juices. P.S. some flash bastards add garlic and saffron to the stock for that South of France flavour and colour.

P.S. Some idiots believe that you can use any quality of wine in cooking because of the temperature change – to put it politely, they are incorrect. One of the great dishes of the world, COQ AU VIN, has been nearly lost by fish-meal-fed chickens and Sicilian Beaujolais!

David Hockney: The Blazer, *July 1970. This is perhaps the most sympathetic of Hockney's many portraits of Peter; it shows him at a time when the first Odin's was an established success, and a year before the ambitions and anxieties of the second Odin's were to change his character.*

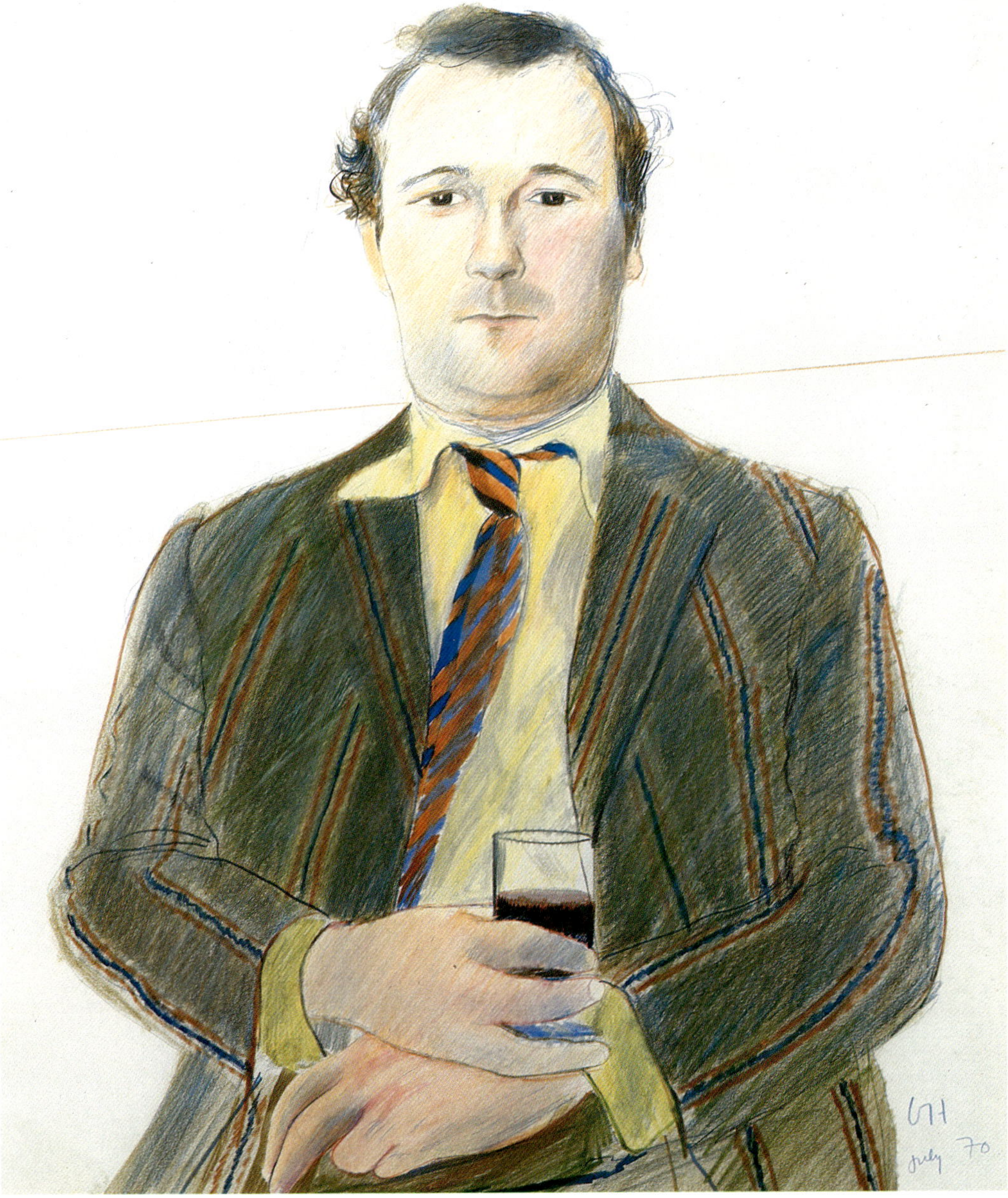
DH
July 70

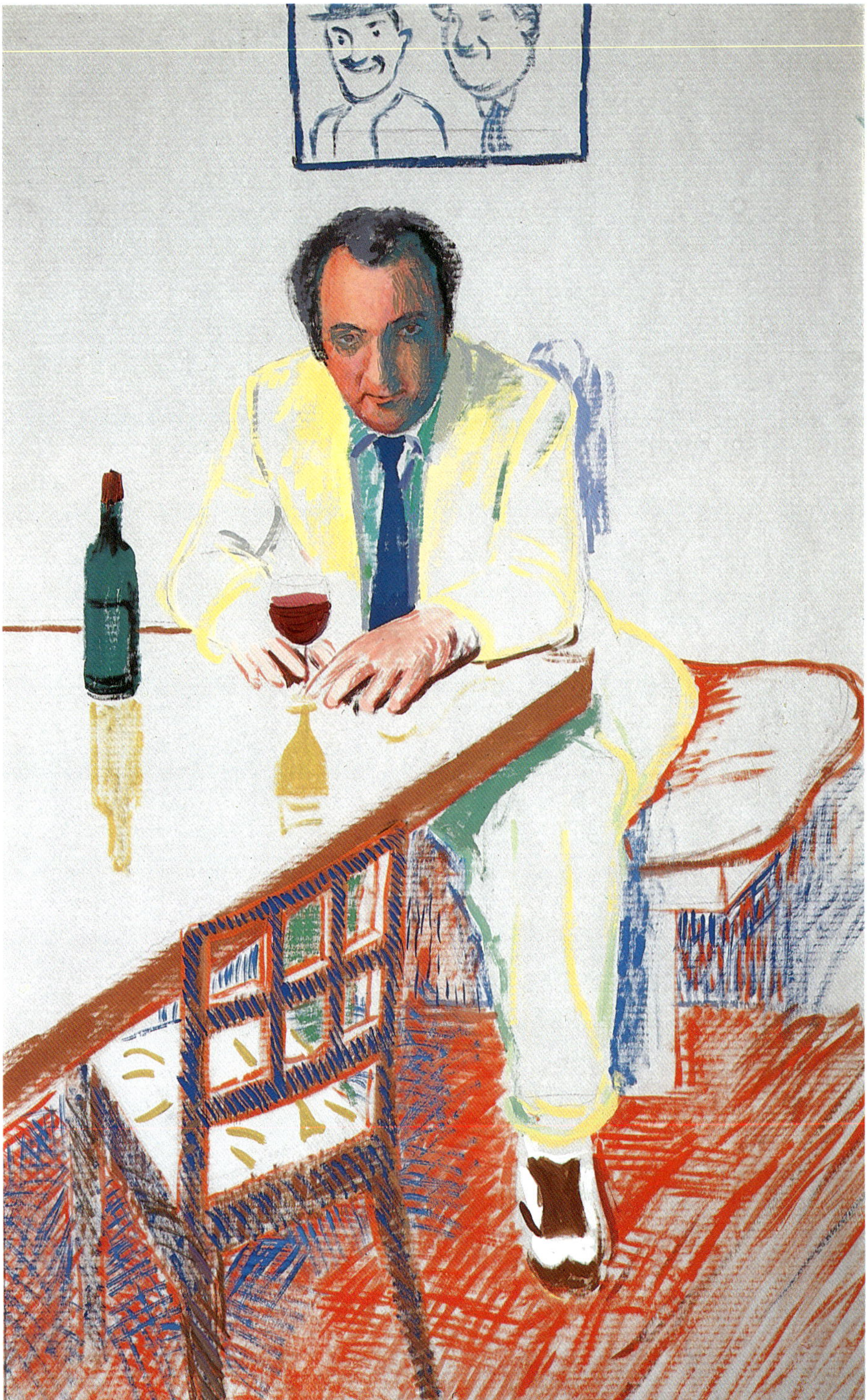

SIMPLE POTATO CAKE

Ingredients:
plain mashed potato
finely chopped cooked crisp cabbage
very finely chopped spring onion

Method:
Just mix some of the cabbage and spring onion into the potato, add salt and pepper, make into patties, fry in a pan until brown on both sides.
 The quantities of this simple little dish are entirely your own.

COLCANNON POTATO

4lbs potatoes
1lb cooked savoy cabbage (crisp)
1oz butter
½ pint of milk
6 chopped spring onions

Peel and boil potatoes. Drain and mash until smooth. Add the spring onions to milk and bring to the boil. Pour onto the potato and beat well until fluffy. Fold in the cabbage with the butter – it is ready.

David Hockney: Peter Langan, *1984. Painted in Los Angeles when Peter was unsuccessfully negotiating with real-estate agents and lawyers in the hope of opening a restaurant there, this picture shows Peter with his face set in a characteristic glower, flushed with alcohol and anger.*

NELL LANGAN'S SOUFFLE OMELETTE

Ingredients
4 egg yolks
4 egg whites
2 dessert spoons of icing sugar
Half a pint of good jam or raspberry purée
A good knob of butter
A miniature bottle of Cointreau

A non stick Teflon pan is the best, but it's by no means essential. Whisk the egg whites until stiff, fold in one dessert spoon of sugar, add the yolks already mixed. The frying pan should be hot, throw in a good knob of butter, it will sizzle but not burn, let it coat the pan, pour in the egg mix, leave on the ring until the base is a light brown, then put it under the pre-heated grill, it will rise swiftly. Remove it, cool the pan base in a tray of cold water, put half the heated purée mixed with half the cointreau in the middle, fold it and then pour the rest casually over the top. Sprinkle in the second dessertspoon of sugar, pour on the rest of the Cointreau and serve direct from the pan. The only reason for cooling the frying pan is that you don't burn off the alcohol which is an optional exotic extra. It is a great treat for children. The little buggers love it.

The Fruit Purée – Buy a packet of frozen raspberries, sweat them over heat with sugar to taste, push through a sieve to remove the pips and heat. Traditional Baked Apples puréed are an ideal filling, use whatever liqueur you feel like.

David Hockney: Peter Langan, October 1969. *Peter is again pictured in the kitchen of the original Odin's. His Löwenbräu, always drunk from a large brandy glass, stands in the right foreground.*

FISH AND VEGETARIAN SOUFFLE OMELETTES

This is exactly the same method as the sweet omelette. Visitors to Brittany always have the omelette St Michel on St Michael's Mount – it's just that instead of jam, you use any fish, crab, lobster, etc. Make a white sauce using a stock made from the crushed bones of the shellfish. Put half of the cooked meat into the yolk and whipped egg whites, season to taste (a marvellous herb to add here is fresh coriander leaf, now available in Greek and Chinese shops and some supermarkets). Cook as before, add the rest of the meat, warmed in a little butter, to the middle fold, and serve sprinkled with chives, chopped spring onions, parsley or whatever you feel like. Pour the sauce over each person's portion. The egg content of this dish remains the same, the meat depends on what your palate desires. There is of course no real need for the additional fillings in the savoury version.

HADDOCK SOUFFLE OMELETTE

My favourite version of this dish and the cheapest, is using Finnan Haddock that had been cooked gently in ½ milk, ½ water. By that I mean just below boiling point. Use the flaked fish having removed the bones. One fish is enough for four people – just use six eggs instead of four. The stock makes a superb base for the simple sauce. Add fresh chopped parsley to the sauce right at the end.

I once knew an old man in Cornwall who swore by Finnan Haddie but smoked haddock produces an excellent result. Serve with boiled potatoes, a salad or a green vegetable.

One of the many vegetarian versions is sautéed sliced mushrooms (very little butter) as the ingredient. Mince or chop finely, half the mushrooms to help spread the flavour amongst the egg mixture – sling in the slices – proceed as normal. Serve with a purée of Spinach, or Tomato, or both.

I am something of a failed vegetarian and later in the book there is a large chapter on vegetarian cuisine with a special emphasis on cooking from the Indian Sub Continent and China.

The variations on a theme of this dish demonstrate that simple ingredients and good taste are the essentials for good eating.

TIPSY CAKE

This is an old Irish favourite said by some to start children on the road to a liking for alcoholic beverages.

1lb Stale Sponge Cake†
4 Tablespoons of Homemade Raspberry Jam or a Fruit Purée
3 Single measures of Whiskey
¼ Pint of Amontillado Style Sherry
¾ Pint Creme Anglaise – use the recipe in the Banana Soufflé
½ Pint Whipped Cream.

†*Peter also used chocolate-chip cookies as the base, claiming that the flavours of chocolate and sherry blend well and give the cake a better bite.*

Method:
Break up the cake roughly, gently mix in the jam or fruit purée. Put in a glass bowl. Mix the sherry and whiskey and sprinkle over the cake, and press it down lightly. Pour the crème anglaise (custard) over the soused cake and chill for a few hours or overnight. Spoon the whipped cream over the top when you want to serve it. Slivered toasted almonds on top add a decorative touch if decoration is required.

HOT BANANA SOUFFLE

This was a post-war favourite when this fruit became popular and inexpensive. All fruit souffles are made in the same way using a basic crème patissière base. The sauces of the souffle are derived from the juices of the fruit added to Creme Anglaise.

1. Basic Creme Patissière:
    ½ Pint of Milk
    4 Egg Yolks
    1 Whole Egg
    1oz Cornflour
    2oz Flour
    5oz Sugar

Method:
1. Boil milk with Vanilla Pod
2. Beat eggs, whole egg, sugar, flour and cornflour together.
3. Pour boiled milk, whisking all the time, (do this slowly), onto the mixed ingredients. Return to the heat, still whisking – it will only take a few seconds for the first bubble to appear. Remove or the eggs will scramble. Pour through sieve into cold container.

2. Ripe Bananas (two)
Blend the bananas in a liquidizer, add ½ the purée to four large tablespoons of Creme Patissière. Whisk 3 egg whites stiff, but not dry, add whites to the banana mixture. Place in souffle dishes measuring *3 inches* already coated with butter and then caster sugar on top. Cook in a pre-heated oven for 15 minutes at Gas Mark 6.

3. The Creme Anglaise
A good souffle should not need a sauce but most people love it, if you like a sauce don't poke the souffle, float it on top and add more as you require.

2½oz Sugar
3 Egg Yolks
¼ Pint Milk
¼ Vanilla Pod or good flavouring.

Method:
Add the sugar to egg yolks, whisk well. Bring milk and vanilla to the boil. Cool slightly, add milk to sugar and egg mix, return to the heat until it thickens. Do not boil, let it cool and in this case add the rest of the banana puree sieved or less if you wish. Store the excess sauce in a fridge.

Both the Creme Patissière and Crème Anglaise will keep, you reheat the Banana Sauce later when required and add the Creme Patissière to your souffle mix when you want to make the souffle the following day. What I mean is: Steps (1) and (3) of this dish can be done ahead.

Exit the myth of the Souffle.

FLOATING ISLANDS

This was my favourite dessert in the early part of my life. As I suppose for most children, the rest of the meal you had to plough through to get to the sweet. This is not the version we had as children. It is the recipe of a cook-writer, restaurant-critic friend of mine – her name is Fay.

Serves 6

6 egg yolks
7oz caster sugar
salt
½ pint single cream
6fl oz creamy (gold top) milk
1 vanilla pod
3 egg whites
1 pint ordinary milk
4oz sugar (for the caramel)

Method:
Combine the yolks, scant 4oz sugar and a pinch of salt in the top of a double saucepan. Heat the cream, creamy milk and vanilla pod in the base saucepan of the double saucepan until it steams. Pour it slowly onto the yolks, whisking all the while. Rinse the base pan, fill with hot simmering water and set on the stove with the yolk mixture above. Cook over simmering water, stirring constantly, until the mixture coats the back of a metal spoon (it thickens also upon cooling). Strain the custard through a sieve or chinois into a shallow dish in which you will serve the floating islands. Set in the fridge.

Near the time of dinner, whisk the 3 egg whites with a pinch of salt to soft peaks. Add the remaining 3oz sugar, a tablespoonful at a time, whisking until the peaks are stiff and glistening. Heat the ordinary milk and enough water to fill a grill pan to a depth of ½ inch/1.25 cm. When it is near boiling, pour it into the grill pan. Float spoonsful of the meringue on the milk and grill under a low to medium heat until they are set and just tinged with brown – a matter of minutes. Lift them out with a slotted spoon and keep them on a large plate, tilted, or in a large colander – they tend to exude liquid.

When it comes to dessert time, pile the meringues prettily onto the custard. Put the 4oz sugar for the caramel into a small heavy bottomed saucepan. Add enough water to wet it thoroughly. Bring it slowly to the boil and, when the sugar is dissolved, boil quickly until the syrup begins to look golden and will spin a thread if dripped from the tines of a fork. Test that you have reached the right point by letting a drop of syrup fall into a cup of cold water. It should set hard. Turn off the heat. Working quickly, and using two forks, weave threads of the caramel and drop splodges of it onto the îles flottantes. Try to spin a shining nest on top but don't worry if all you get is brittle droplets – they will give the requisite crunch. Take to the table. You cannot do the sugar work much before dessert time as it quickly softens and loses the point.

He omits the recipe for Mrs Langan's Chocolate Pudding, a dessert invented by his mother that was on the menu of the first Odin's in 1966, and is still on the menu of the second Odin's in 1990. He once showed me how to make it. Separate the yolks of a dozen eggs and slowly mix them with 4 oz. of caster sugar – under no circumstances whip them; when they are blended, fold in 3 oz. of Bourneville cocoa. Beat the whites of egg to a froth and then pour into them the mixed yolks, and stir – the froth should be much reduced but not wholly flattened. The mixture should then be put into a large shallow baking tin lined with greaseproof paper that has been well buttered and floured, and baked on the middle shelf of the oven for between 15 and 20 minutes, depending on the depth of the pudding – it must NOT be allowed to dry, but must remain soggy and malleable, and if the needle is withdrawn clean the pudding is ruined. Let the cooked pudding cool. Melt an 8-oz. bar of Cadbury's Bourneville Chocolate, gently beat a pint of double cream, spread both evenly on the pudding, and then gently roll it, using the greaseproof paper for even leverage.

By calling it Mrs Langan's Chocolate Pudding, Peter, in the use of 'Mrs', unwittingly challenged the chocolate pudding made by Mrs Beeton (the only other famous cook known by that simple title), a meagre confection of cake crumbs and vanilla essence that must be eaten with custard, and conjured comfortable visions of his own domestic life, well fed and feet up by the fire; it was a much more successful ploy than giving it his own name, or some Frenchified nonsense. Peter loathed English custard.

CHAPTER 2

Castleknock College

THE FORMATIVE YEARS

THE YOUNG PUP HAS TO BE HOUSE TRAINED

My first night in an alien no mans land the tears and the fear of a dog that had always been free to roam, was now caged in a large kennel called a dormitory with thirty strangers and three hundred others I had yet to encounter my childhood had ended from that night onwards there were to be four seasons in every year – summertime had gone forever.

THE RITUALS OF MY ALCATRAZ

My old, twice removed gran aunt in Clarecastle told me that this dump would put god into me. She was a religious maniac and had always suspected me of leaning on my grandmothers till. My fear of god and hell developed into a devout disbelief in the son of a bitch, that someone I couldnt see was three persons in one – The Holy ghost being a bloody dove. Anyway the only time I was going to meet him was after my demise, a somewhat nebulous assignation.

The public utterances to the deity ocurred fifteen times a day, bells summoned you to class and prayer or both and of course to the refectory for the course inedible foddor.

I lived in my own private world a hermit in the company of three hundred strangers. (These notes to be developed into humourous and absurd incidents over the next five and a half years.)

MY SECRET LIFE AT SCHOOL
MORNING PLEASURES
IN THE WOODWORK ROOM

This haven of happiness was at the back of St Mary's dormitory. The maids, known as skivvies kept their cleaning materials in a cupboard beside the woodwork room which was at the back of St Mary's dorm.

In the early fifties Holy Mass was obligatory for everyone every day and twice on Saints Days and Feast Days. If however you had a cold or bad headaches (of which I had more than my fair share) you were permitted a "lie in" which meant you stayed in bed while everybody else went to mass.

There was a long mirror down the length of the dormitory with beds on either side which meant that the deaf and dumb skivvies from Cabra College cleaning the washing bowls could easily observe discreetely any careless late rising youth without turning their back. The art of dressing was as follows.

You dropped your pyjama bottoms first to put on your underpants over which you took an inordinate amount of time, the top only came to your waist anyway, then the girl could see your teenage totem pole being given a little morning exercise.

Contact was soon made and social meetings took place immediately after breakfast in the woodwork room, my nickname was "King of the Woodwork". The priests thought this suitable therapy for a rather odd little boy, so my presence in that vicinity was considered quite normal.

These were some of the most wonderful appreciative women I have ever met, they were not shy and two at a time was often the norm. Communication was a problem – I bought an EVER READY battery, put it in a sock in my cupboard and indicated that when I was wanted they took it out of the sock and placed it upon the shelf, that battery shed more light and love than the manufacturers ever dreampt of.

A post breakfast check every morning meant my teenage erections found plenty of freedom. Word got round the deaf and dumb vine and they exchanged dormitories. I had seven different girls including what the americans might call a near senior citizen.

They were game for everything except insertion. Memories of those first naked contacts with rampant women still floods this ageing engine with immediate pleasure.

There were of course near disasters, clothes were hung in the cupboard and because they were deaf and I was excited, two of us were nearly caught one day and were sardined in the bloody cupboard without enough room to put our clothes on silently, late for class I spent the morning under the prefect's bed and appeared at lunchtime.

In that institution I learned guile, cunning and forgery†. In my last year there were few but fulfilling encounters. They changed the location of the woodwork room and we were only able to meet accross the road in Lord Iveagh's estate his swimming pool was always empty of water – there was never anyone in the big house and of course who would ever dream of finding an arcangel like myself and two sweet girls from Cabra College carousing in the rotting leaves of an empty swimming pool. (This is a very rough semi-complete paragraph of my first encounter with the gates of heaven)

†*The reference to forgery in the context of his schooldays and no others is disingenuous. He tolerated the forgery of signature paintings sold in the art gallery next door to the first Odin's, and when he asked me to bring Tom Keating to the second Odin's he treated him with kindness and respect, and made it clear that he held in contempt those dealers and museum officials who had been duped by Tom's* Sexton Blakes *(Tom's euphemism for his imitations of Samuel Palmer). In an article on collecting, Peter observed, 'I have known pictures purchased by unscrupulous dealers to appear six months later with signatures which were certainly not there the day they were bought at auction.' Making a kindred assertion over dinner at the Brasserie, he was challenged to change the signature on one of his own pictures and put it through Sotheby's, to which his response was 'Bugger that, but I'll write some James Joyce, and you can put that through Sotheby's.' He always maintained that he had successfully composed a draft connected with* Finnegans Wake, *not by imitation, but by ESP, letting loose his*

Patrick Procktor: Still Life of Flowers in a Coffee Pot, *1974. Peter wished to use this as a menu cover and went so far as to have a reproduction printed before realising that it was the wrong shape and that he could not print over the image. Very few trial prints survive.*

subconscious to work with what he could recall of the book, and that this manuscript had then, in spite of its modern ink and dissimilarities of handwriting, been sold at Sotheby's for well over a thousand pounds – a price much in line with the market then current. From the limited information given in American Book Prices Current *it is impossible to determine which manuscript, if any, is Peter's, or whether some distorting embellishments crept into the tale that relieve Sotheby's of responsibility for accepting a forgery as genuine.*

Late in life, and utterly cynical about the art market, Peter amused himself by scribbling signatures and dedications on exhibition posters, almost always with a ball-point pen so that no sane man should be deceived – but some were. He asked me, long after Picasso's death in 1972 and with the poster of a posthumous exhibition in his hand, whether the old man would have addressed him as Peter *or* Pierre, *and which way the accent sloped on* chère; *I told him that I did not know, but that* chère *with an accent was an improbable endearment as it is the feminine form – Peter's inability to speak French had already cost him dear.*

THOSE SIX LONELY YEARS

I am often asked the question why those six years were so important to me. The answer is simple and applies to both women and men who went to boarding schools after the war and in the early fifties, you arrived as a child and left as an adult and in all those years you were still treated as an ignoramus, beckoned by bells and controlled by a God invented by man in his own image and likeness because he cannot face the finality of his own death.

The old saying that whoever invented the expression Homo Sapiens was a bit of a prick is true, animals fight to feed and protect themselves whereas we kill each other shrouded in the veil of armour of one bloody god or another.

(The section on formative years in college will concentrate on other things besides my hatred of HOLIFICAL INVENTION.)

The final day came near and my spirits grew with dreams of women and freedom. Father Walsh by now the President asked me to his office for the final goodbye to Castleknock and hello to life

"Well Peter the priesthood is out of the question" he said in what seemed to be soliloquy

"Yes father"

"There's no need for you to reply to what was meant as polite observation. I suppose you'll be glad to be leaving us after all these years after all you never joined in."

"Yes father I am glad to be going"

"Where are you going to"?

"England Father"

"To England indeed well we are relieved at your departure our disrespect for each other, is I am sure mutual.

"Yes Father thank you very much"

He got up from behind his desk, his eyes seemed dark and dead behind his heavy rimmed glasses he held out his hand

"Good luck Peter – Father O'Donaghue (the Dean, my enemy of nearly six years standing) seems to think that you will land on your feet. Be safe!"

"Thank you goodbye Father."

As the car passed through the front gates for the last time, I stopped the chauffer, Peter and peed two pints of tea on to the stone supports. It was a dry day and I could see from a gently flowing stream that mine was not an original comment.

The priests of Castleknock meant well but as they had never learned how to live, how could they know how to teach

CHAPTER 3

Findlaters

MY LAST FEW MONTHS IN IRELAND

My first job was with Findlaters, importers, wholesalers and retailers of food, wine and spirits. My wages were two pounds ten shillings a week I only spent a few months there this chapter will describe a dying firm living in yesterdays world even in those days of the fifties. Dermot Findlater was too old and his son Alex too young. Theirs was a firm of great style, but also an endangered species. The days of the gentleman businessman catering to a class that no longer existed had gone forever.

DUBLIN MEMORIES

I would like to concentrate on the city at this time of my life as an outsider because when we as a family moved to Dublin, I was at boarding school most of the time and then I left for England months after school, but a young outside mind can observe what locals take for granted. The great restaurants are now all gone but I can remember their dishes and the fifties when the Irish had money for the grand life for the first time ever.

A new noveau riche wanting to be sophisticated was born this to be written about the people. A Mercedes became the emblem of success. etc.

I read my first cookbook BE BOLD IN YOUR KITCHEN and was fascinated by the authors love for eating good food.

There will be twenty recipes in this third chapter, mostly very simple with a leaning towards fish.

I will end this chapter with my thoughts on a country I knew I was not going back to and my mind being set on the hopes that the girls of England were more sociably inclined toward mutual satisfaction than their Irish counterparts.

Ron Kitaj: Foreplay, *circa 1974. Inscribed 'for Peter and food', this was one of many drawings, prints and paintings collected by Peter on an exchange basis from Kitaj, Procktor and Hockney, with the artists 'eating them down'. Peter chose to hang it in the reception area of the second Odin's as a challenge to any Mrs Grundy among his patrons.*

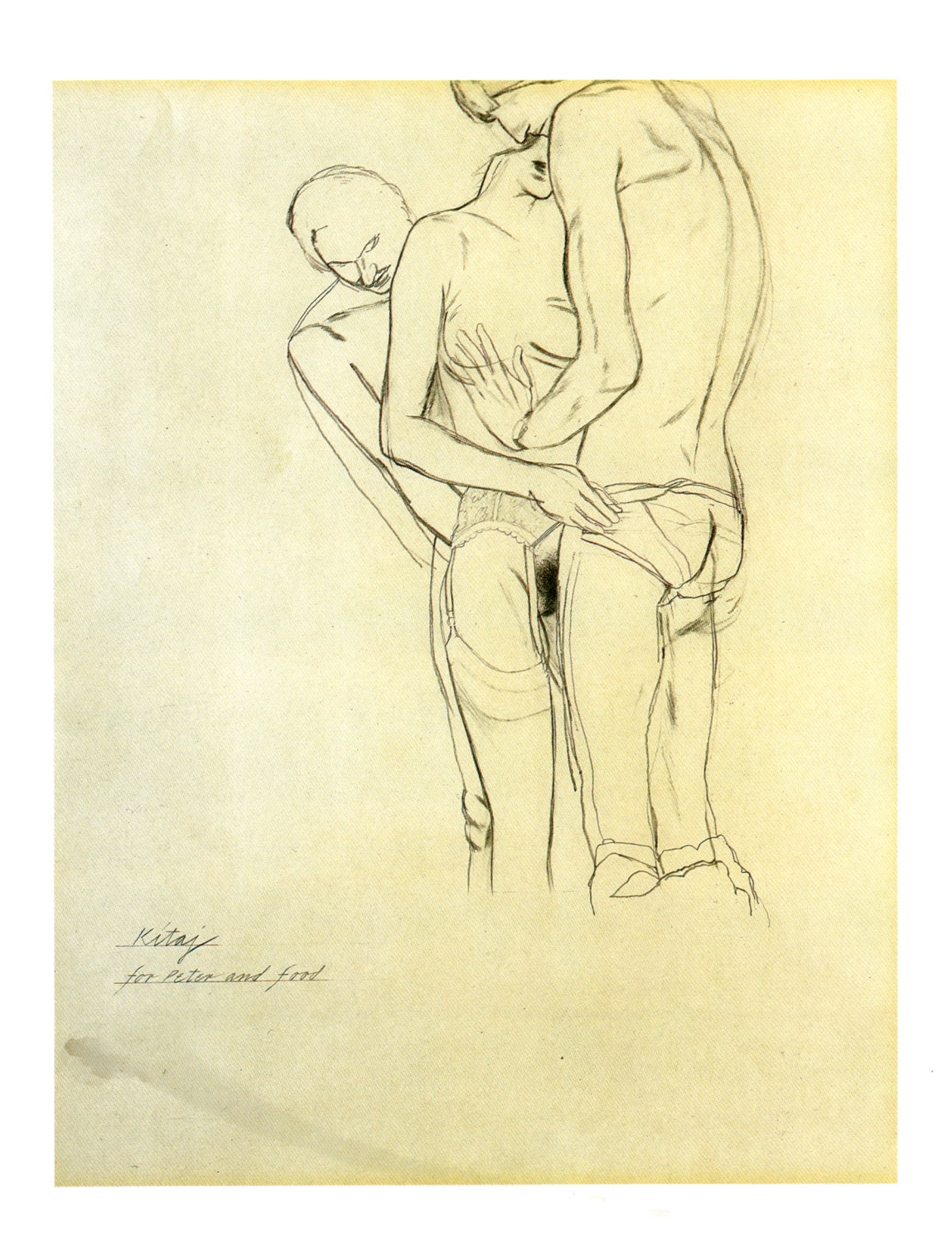

Kitaj
for Peter and food

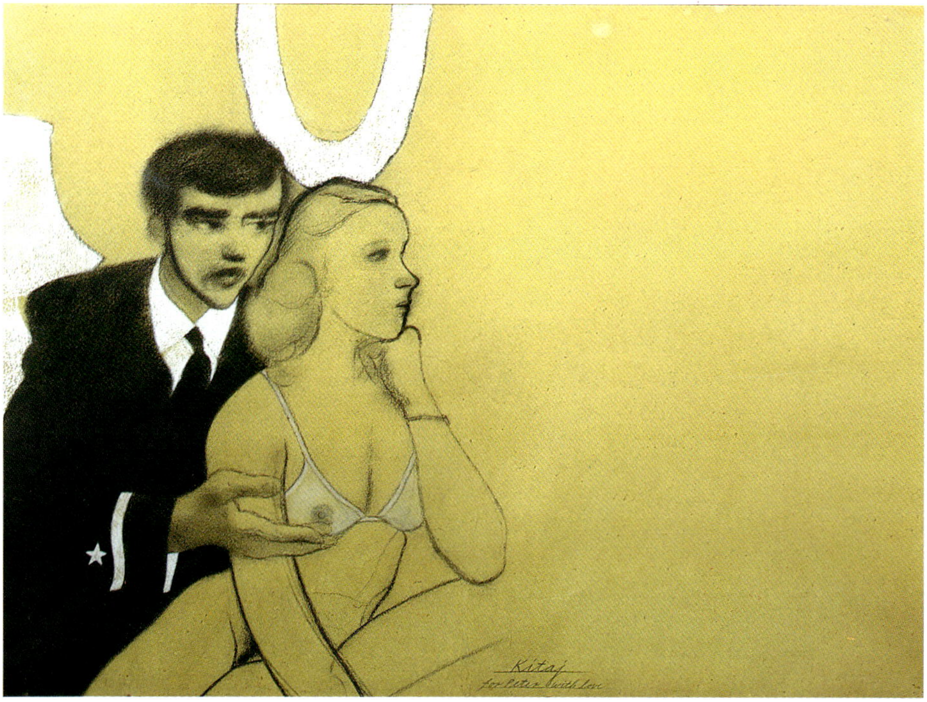
Kitaj

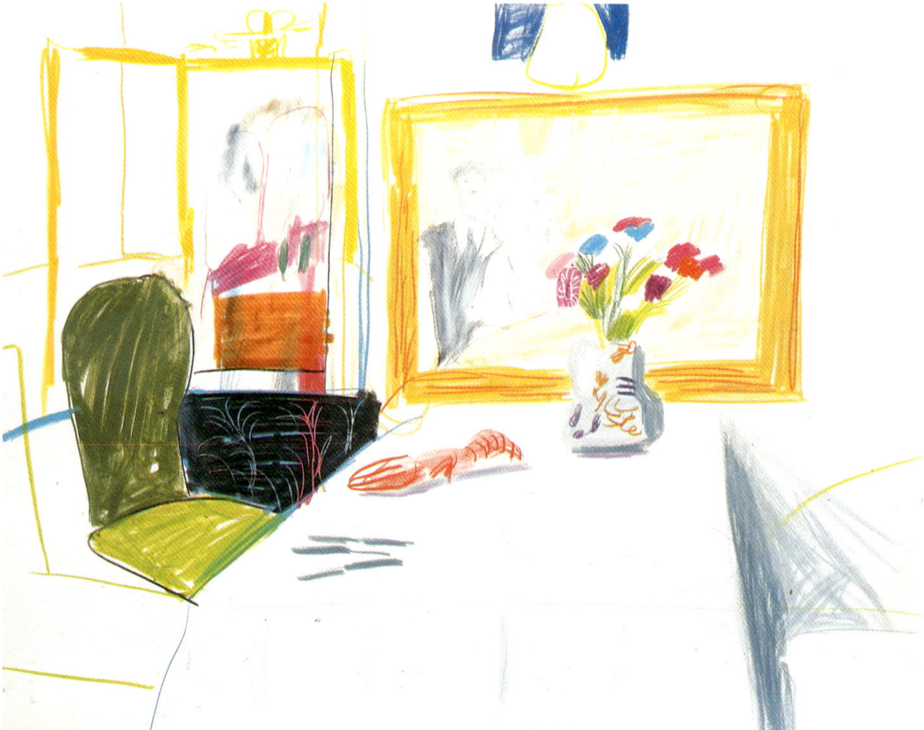

CHAPTER 4

My Parents

I want to write about my parents at this stage of the book because this was the time I went to England. It was obvious to me that I was leaving home forever.

Behind me was a world I would I could never exist in, my mother was ill. I was running away – There was a tear in the corner of the Saturday Evening Post.

I read Arthur Millers play Death Of a Salesman long before I saw it on the stage, it frightened me it depicts the antithesis of Norman Rockwell's view of the happiness of the successfull middle class.

My father a salesman was a winner, but at a price. He only knew how to win, a weakness I suffer from myself. My mother died from Multiple Sclerosis after a long ilness. I have one brother John.

This chapter will again be incidents in our lives until I left home and then the feeling of emptyness I have now that they are both gone.

Narrative sample: – He polished his motor all day with Simonez, it

TOP: *Ron Kitaj:* The Sailor and the Girl, *circa 1974.*
BOTTOM: *A view within the second Odin's by David Hockney, showing how Peter placed the Kitaj drawing.*

looked new to me, he was selling it and getting his first company car. I remember his eyes bright with happiness and excitement and what I now know to be ambition. Strangely, I remember what he said to my mother –

"I'm going to be top man,"

she replied "come in for gods sake it's tea time".

I was six years old.

I often wonder why that day still lives with me, if the offspring of a stallion have the strengths and weaknesses of the parent then I am my fathers son. (Sample finish)

This chapter to also tell the stories of the lighter side of the petroleum trade in Ireland.

There are to be no recipes for this chapter.

CHAPTER 5

England The Early Years

I think this is complete enough in the details given below. It covers my arrival in England – Sunderland to be precise.

It has amusing moments mostly about women whose husbands were often away for months on end leaving behind randy wives with an eye for petrol pump attendants like myself.

One particular incident comes to mind, when I was riding a women who was the local bike – everyone was poking her. Unfortunately two of her husbands friends mistook me for her regular lover and threw me through the first floor bedroom window of this brand new estate in South Shields, they kicked the glass out first with yours truly stark naked in hot pursuit. They were social workers they slung my clothes out after me including her knickers and bra. I spent the somewhat bruised night in a telephone box.

She came in that morning to the filling station "Where's me bra and panties. "You are going to pay for the window aren't you?, glass costs brass you know."

I got suddenly ill and left town, after that I was always ill when South Shields came into the conversation at the Sunderland Depot.

Anecdotal little stories like these including one superb dinner in Durham Town. The rest of this chapter is about high life living on a low income. The business of catering starts in this chapter and my life goes from the North East to London then Cornwall and my Regent Oil Company Waterloo in Somerset.

I return to London and the restaurant trade begins with Kirsten Benson at Odins, she was about to go bankrupt. I convinced her to keep the restaurant open, I became a salesman for Aer Lingus in London, I would check in at nine o'clock in the morning in Regent St and leave to cook at ODINS – I return in the evening to check out and then leave to cook dinner at the restaurant. I leave Aer Lingus and go into partnership with Kirsten at ODINS.

Now it all begins at last after years of dreams I am in the restaurant business. Twenty recipes in this section and stories from this part of my life – I was just eighteen when I arrived in Sunderland and I was twenty three when I turned ODINS around.

Kirsten was right there was no money. I went back to my part time snooping business for ten days in June 1966. Twenty recipes

Part One: The North-East, their loving women and jealous husbands.
            The people – unemployment, honesty.
            Insert in middle of text some northern recipes.
Part Two: London, at last.
            The restaurants and the obsession that has never left me – the restaurant trade.
            Part time snooping for extra money, amusing but dangerous moments, i.e. visit to Naples.
Part Three: The Cornwall salesman for Regent Oil Company.
            Private catering.
            Randy.
            Twenty-four hour days.
            Dealing in carriage clocks.
            Not selling anything.
            Transferred to Somerset – eventually fired.
Part Four: Return to London – an Aer Lingus salesman for eight weeks the I walked into Odins in Devonshire Street.
            Recipes
            Cornwall cooking.

ODINS

Starters

Callans Combinations — 9/6
frogs legs and snail starter

Odins Spare Ribs — 6/6

Pâté en Brioche — 6/6
our own pâté in brioche - hot

Winter Soup — 4/6
a red wine game soup

A Mussel Soup — 6/6

Oyster Clare — 9/6
hot oysters, different flavours, a very light starter

Main Dishes

Rib of Beef Plain or Peppered — 17/6
a wing rib steak cooked to order

Roast Pheasant — 21/-
in a burgundy sauce

Prawn and Scallop Odin — 21/-
cooked the same way as the lobster was in summer — fresh shellfish, brandy, cream

Peppered Pigeon Breasts

Plain Fillets of Lamb
grilled in herbs and butter

Sirloin Steak Langan — 17/6
in a light mustard and cream sauce

Rack of Lamb — 15/6

Breast of Chicken — 14/6
chicken, apples, almonds and mushrooms

Roast Duck — 18/6
half a duck in a fruit sauce

Fillet of Pork — 14/6
undecided ?

Vegetables 5/-
a choice of any two of the following:-

Red cabbage. Colcannon Potatoes. Ratatouille.
French Beans. Rice. Jacket Potatoes. Mixed Salad.
Green Salad. Tomato and Onion Salad.

Sweets

Mrs Langan's Chocolate Pudding — 6/6

Lemon Sorbet — 5/-

Apricot Vilag — 6/6

Cold Cointreau Soufflé — 7/6

Vicars Folly — 6/6

per person 2/-

An Odin's menu with several of Peter's own recipes including Apricot Vilag and Mrs Langan's Chocolate Pudding.

<u>Odins – The Beginning</u> at 26 Devonshire Street.   <u>Chapter 6</u> (Ideas etc.)

Part One: The funeral crisis.
"Peter you can stand in the shadow of the sun".
A visit to Paris – my partner never knew about.
The reward – £1200 – dreams become nightmares.

CHAPTER 6

Odins

A FIGHT FOR SURVIVAL

There is a boozer at the end of Manchester Street in London, when I first lived in London in 1960 my abode was a grotty little bedsit at thirty two Manchester Street.

I met a man at the pub who put me onto an easy money maker it involved following people about and writing a report about their activities, it was usually suspicious wives or husbands worrying about strayed loved ones, it was very boring but provided much needed cash to indulge my penchant for expensive restaurants.

They were often visiting Americans which I found rather odd, mine was not to reason why just to do the job and collect the money. There were amusing moments. On one occasion I had to traipse round after two very respectable Americans, they were both married and it seems one of their wives wanted to check on her "ladies man" husband. They were being unfaithful to their wives but not to each other – I gave them a very clean sheet report.

I stopped doing this part time work when I became a salesman in Cornwall. It was now 1966 I had returned to London and had been involved in Odins for several weeks.

Kirsten lived by complete coincidence at 26 Manchester Street, we were discussing our cash problem, she was making supper for her children, it was a Sunday I slipped out for a pint, there in the same bar was dear old Oliver.

I told him my troubles just by way of conversation.

"Well old darling I've got a job for you, pots of money dear, but you may get shot".

"You are joking?

"No I'm not"

It seemed absurd I asked him what had happened to the good old days of the odd divorce or two, oh Yes he still did that but then he reminded me that it was not fifty pounds I was short of.

"Think of it sweet, a week's work – no sleep I'll give you pills, a week's work," he repeated – four hundred pounds expenses, twelve hundred for yourself and you can save that rat hole of a restaurant". He intimated that as far as he could ascertain the gentleman seemed to be a dangerous american subject to sudden changes of mood. "You wont be breaking any law Peter he will, you move well you can stand in the shadow of the sun." I wondered whether I would be collecting what was then the equivalent of a years salary.

I took the job and was booked into the Hyde Park Hotel and the Cumberland the next six days were dull, he did not go shopping and walked from one hotel to the other. He always walked everywhere, he seemed to have nothing to do, then he went to Air France.

I was right behind him, he spoke softly but the clerk's voice was clear, she repeated the flight number the time and hoped he would have a pleasant flight tomorrow, she thanked him in the name he used at both hotels, there were queues at all the reservation stations he did not seem to notice me.

I booked the same flight there were seats, there was one snag, I lost him for an hour, while I was getting my ticket he slipped me. I booked an earlier flight on BEA as well just in case. Oliver contacted me I gave him all the information he arranged cars for me in Paris. The American checked out of the Cumberland first but left his luggage to be collected.

Porters and clerks always seem to be deaf, they repeat the name given, very audibly. I had already checked out of both hotels. He walked to the Hyde Park, checked out identical luggage left for the airport, so did I. Oliver was informed by me of the name of the luggage collector at the Cumberland.

We travelled near each other to Paris. I cleared customs quickly and waited he travelled by taxi to a hotel off the Champs Elysee.

There were more vacant rooms in the hotel I telephoned my contact number offered to in book myself, the man said No but I did advise him that the name used was still the same. I was told to outside Fauchon the following morning at ten o clock with two shopping bags in my right hand.

I was there early, at the precise time a small man approached me. "Your name Langan"? "Yes". "You have a friend in London, what is his name?" "Oliver" he then handed me an envelope and walked away.

Dull and routine, I stayed in Paris for two days, on the third day there was a report in the third page of *The Tribune* of a body found in that hotel of an American, foul play was suspected – I did not go to the police, I did not want to become the dead mans roomate. I honestly had no idea I was endangering anybody's life other than my own.

It was strange that I was paid in Paris and not by Oliver, my own assumption tells me that as I was ignorant of everything it was easier to pay me than kill me. I only knew him by one name and no one will ever know it but me. Oliver said on my return, "I see you made it darling". "Are you surprised you bastard?" "Yes my buttercup I am, have a lager on me"†.

---

†*On his first page Peter wrote 'I have not felt like telling the story of how Odins survived its financial crisis of 1966 until now', but here, in telling it, he withheld the crucial details that make sense of the episode and his subsequent behaviour; this is not altogether surprising, for had the whole truth been published in his lifetime, dear old Oliver's warning 'But you may get shot' would almost certainly have been realised. The American murdered in Paris was involved in fund-raising and arms-running for the IRA. Peter knew this, but he did not know the identity of the agency that hired him – he assumed it to be MI5 or Special Branch; he also assumed that he had been hired because he was expendable – if he were identified and killed by the IRA, his death would merely be attributed to some internecine quarrel within the organisation, or to vengeance on a supposed informer. He knew that his life was in jeopardy, but the payment of £1,200 was at least as much as he could earn in a year as a clerk for Aer Lingus, and whatever he did not spend of the £400 expenses was a by no means despicable bonus.*

He failed to take into account the quality of fear. For quite two years after the assassination could not decide whether greater safety lay in his behaving decorously or flamboyantly, in being more or less identifiably Irish. In the end he decided that conspicuous behaviour would save his kneecaps or his life, but he was long convinced that a bomb would be lobbed through the door of little Odin's, and when we first looked at the premises of the larger restaurant he wondered what would happen if the windows were subject to bomb blast. In 1979, another event, one that had nothing to do with him, again triggered the recollection and the fear. In some curious way he felt that a sinister part of the British Establishment had hold on him, and that if ever he offended, information about the Paris assassination would quietly pass to the IRA. In 1988, when he was writing this autobiographical fragment shortly before his death, the fear was still so prominent in his mind that of only three finished chapters one dealt with the assassination, and he concluded the narrative with '... sleep however over two decades later is shallow and many of my dreams are nightmares.'

I paid off the suppliers, changed wine merchants and had enought money to remove the junk off the walls and begin to develop what is now known as the Langan look. Kerstin never knew about anything as far as she was concerned the takings were better each week.

It is true I had broken no law, I had half expected not to survive, the coin just landed on the other side. Odins as it is now was born out of an inevitable tragedy that had nothing to do with me, sleep however over two decades later is shallow and many of my dreams are nightmares.

(This is a first rough about the beginnings of ODINS.)

The second part will tell the story of the success there will be thirty recipes.

Part Two: The love, fun, freedom and the ambition of a hard man who would win at any cost.
The silenced purveyors
The cooking begins.
I redesign the restaurant.
The Hockney, Procktor, Kitaj, Francis Bacon club with acolytyes dive.
Oldenburg, Stella, etc., turned it into a Cafeteria Royal of the sixties.
The literati loved it too – Osborne, Levin, Waterhouse, etc.‡

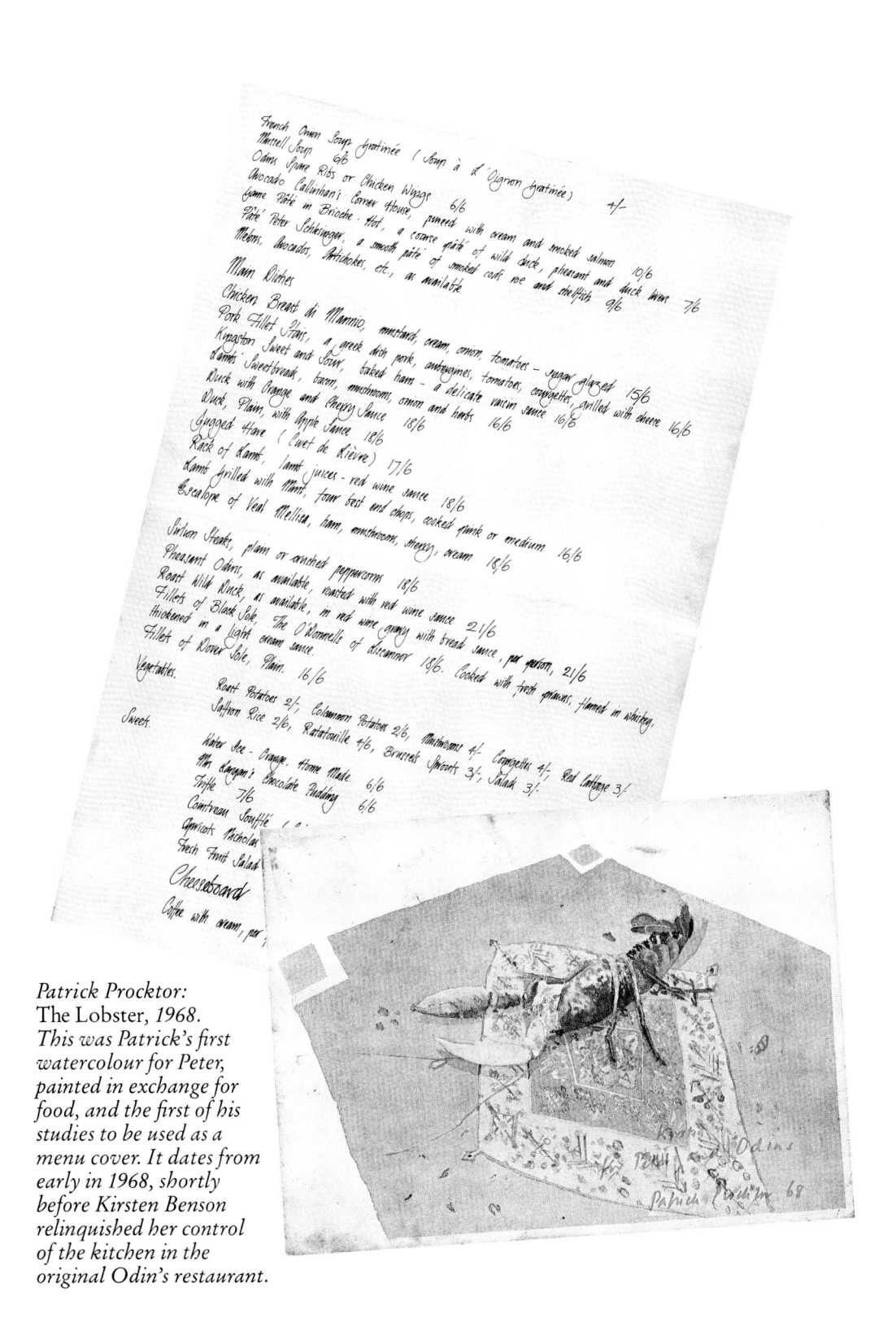

French Onion Soup Gratinée (Soupe à l'Oignon Gratinée) 4/-
Mussel Soup 6/6
Odin's Spare Ribs or Chicken Wings 6/6
Avocado Callinhan's Corner House, pureed with cream and smoked salmon 10/6
Game Pâté in Brioche - Hot, a coarse pâté of wild duck, pheasant and duck livers
Pâté Peter Schlesinger, a smooth pâté of smoked cods roe and shellfish 9/6 7/6
Melons, Avocados, Artichokes, etc., as available

Main Dishes

Chicken Breast di Marino, mustard, cream, onion, tomatoes - sugar glazed 15/6
Pork Fillet Spais, a greek dish, pork, aubergines, tomatoes, courgettes 16/6
Kingston Sweet and Sour, baked ham - a delicate raisin sauce 16/6
Lamb Sweetbreads, bacon, mushrooms, onion and herbs, grilled with cheese 16/6
Duck with Orange and Cherry Sauce 18/6
Duck, Plain, with Apple Sauce 16/6
Jugged Hare (Civet de Lièvre) 17/6
Rack of Lamb, lamb juices - red wine sauce 18/6
Lamb grilled with Ullmi, four best end chops, cooked pink or medium 16/6
Escalope of Veal Mellica, ham, mushrooms, sherry, cream 18/6
Sirloin Steaks, plain or crushed peppercorn 18/6
Pheasant Odin, as available, roasted with red wine sauce 21/6
Roast Wild Duck, as available, in red wine gravy with bread sauce, per person 21/6
Fillets of Black Sole, The O'Donnells of Ascommon 19/6. Cooked with fresh prawns, flamed in whiskey, thickened in a light cream sauce
Fillet of Dover Sole, Plain. 16/6

Vegetables:
Roast Potatoes 2/-, Colcannon Potatoes 2/6, Mushrooms 4/-, Courgettes 4/-, Red Lettuce 3/-
Saffron Rice 2/6, Ratatouille 4/6, Brussels Sprouts 3/-, Salads 3/-

Sweet.
Water Ice - Orange, Home Made. 6/6
Mrs Keegan's Chocolate Pudding 6/6
Trifle 7/6
Cointreau Soufflé
Apricots Nicholas
Fresh Fruit Salad
Cheeseboard
Coffee with cream, per

Patrick Procktor:
The Lobster, *1968.*
This was Patrick's first watercolour for Peter, painted in exchange for food, and the first of his studies to be used as a menu cover. It dates from early in 1968, shortly before Kirsten Benson relinquished her control of the kitchen in the original Odin's restaurant.

‡*Soon after the larger Odin's opened, still heavily in debt, Peter was asked to provide for an agreed fee a banquet for the last night of a John Osborne play at the Royal Court Theatre. He did so, and did it very well, taking so much care with its richness and presentation that its cost was not covered by the fee. He was content to cover the loss, seeing the banquet as an exercise that must enhance his reputation and bring custom to the restaurant, but he was not content to accept delay in payment; months passed, and his bills and increasingly abusive telephone calls were ignored; convinced at last that those who had commissioned the banquet did not intend to pay for it, he cooked the last covers for Odin's, took a taxi to Sloane Square, told the driver to wait for him in Holbein Place, smashed as many of the theatre's glass doors as he could, and returned to Odin's in the cab.*

He claimed that he had kicked in the doors, but I never knew him to wear shoes or boots suitable for such a dangerous undertaking, and thought it more likely that he taken a meat cleaver or tenderising mallet from the kitchen; apart from this detail I had no reason to disbelieve the tale, told often enough as I have told it, until 2 October 1987, when Peter wrote 'Langan Turns the Tables' for the Evening Standard; *there he adds the gloss that one of the guests at the party stole a vase from the restaurant, splitting a pair that if still matched would now be worth thousands of pounds, and neuters the second and more amusing half of the story and its real point. In this revised version it seems that Peter went to the theatre at two in the morning, found the offending artistic director in a haze of cannabis, and merely threatened to smash the glass doors; a cheque arrived by motorcycle messenger the following day.*

This discrepancy raises a serious problem with many of Peter's self-portraying tales, for unless they were published, and thus passed by libel lawyers, they were, even at their most consistent and unvarying, likely to have been a little adjusted, embroidered and embellished to enhance his amour-propre. His reference below to 'the real Royal Court story', in the knowledge that his written version had recently been published, may suggest that he planned a third version.

The restaurant was now successful and in 1968 a man called Quentin Crewe came and made me a legend in my own lunchtime.

ODINS AS IT IS NOW – 27 DEVONSHIRE STREET

This was the emergence in myself of a natural animal who would always take any risk to achieve what I wanted provided it harmed no one. For the first time I fully understood and remembered my father's expression all those years ago when he was polishing his old motor, then I was like a golfer on a winning streak, all those eight foot putts dropped.

The chapter will be about the pressures to begin with, the pleasure in the middle and the return of the ambition of expression at the end. There will be approximately 40 recipes.
The pressure of opening a luxury restaurant under capitalised.
The real Royal Court story.
Story of the opening night.
Closing little Odins end of a Friday night – opening Odins next door for Saturday supper.

The young years had gone forever, now the sixties were over I had to be a little business like.

I bought a picture instead of a roof over my head, etc. etc. The best were sold in the crash of the early seventies – fiddled of twenty thousand pounds by a French wine merchant.†

†*The wine merchant's 'fiddle' was less a deception on his part than a confusion on Peter's, caused by his inabilty to speak French. The association of Jean-Marc Moussis and Peter was celebrated in a drawing by David Hockney in Paris in the summer of 1975; as that drawing was for many years used as a menu cover in the larger Odin's, it is impossible to believe that Peter was cheated by Moussis, for the vengeful side of his nature would have compelled him to destroy such daily reminders of his humiliation. He was, nevertheless, unwilling to humiliate himself by admitting that he was in any way to blame for his predicament, and his rage on discovering the catastrophic consequences of his simple error was directed at Moussis alone. In spite of this adjustment of the truth, there was, as in most such cases, an obvious clue to the reality, and here it lay in the original drawing, still hanging in Odin's, and in its continued use as a menu cover.*

Much of the summer of 1975 was spent in France, and part in Paris, where, with the sculptor Michael Goldman and his wife (a black dancer), he trawled the best restaurants, eating and drinking extravagantly, running up bills as high as a thousand pounds for dinner. Through Goldman he met Moussis, who told him of a small vineyard to which he had exclusive access, that had produced a modest quantity of an exquisite white wine that he wished to sell in a single bargain. Peter did not find it so exquisite, but decided that it would do well enough as a house white of good quality for Odin's, and was excited by the notion that he might commission David Hockney to design the label. Moussis spoke no English and Peter no French; drinking the while, each spoke his own language very slowly to the other, each thought he had been understood, the bargain was struck, and, the best of friends, the two men continued their prodigal round of the best restaurants.

It was only when the first delivery of wine reached the English Customs that Peter realised that he was the victim of an error and had bought not 3,000 bottles but 30,000. The wine was to be paid for when it reached England, and as consignment after consignment had to be cleared through Customs, Peter became desperate to raise ready cash and had to sell pictures to meet demands for some £20,000 more than he had expected to pay. He had nowhere to store so much wine, and as case after case was unloaded onto the pavement of Devonshire Street, felt like the Sorcerer's Apprentice; the landlord of The Prince Regent, a public house just round the corner of Marylebone High Street to which Peter often repaired if the atmosphere in Odin's became tense and disagreeable, cleared a basement and housed most of it. Worse was to come: the exquisite wine was useless as a house white – it had not travelled well, did not last well, and became so sweet that it could only be sold by the glass as a dessert wine – and that at a time when dessert wines were despised and unfashionable. Even the label was a disaster – Hockney did not design it, dashing Peter's hopes that he might be able to sell cases of the accursed brew as Christmas presents, and the young man who did misspelled Peter's name.

Visits to France, dinners at Pere Bise, Hotel la Cote D'or with Michael Goldman and Chef Minot – days in Haut Savoy – evenings in Paris.

CHAPTER 7

Langans Brasserie

THE BEGINNING 1976

As a nickname I prefer "an SIONNACH GLIC" to "The man who stands in the shadow of the sun," the former means a cunning fox. My wife reminds me that although "foxes bite chickens necks, hounds catch them and farmers shoot them – they never die of old age."

This may be true, everyone said opening a restaurant the size of the Brasserie was madness and that the old Coq D'Or† would finally bury the arrogant mick. These were fellow trade proprietors who did not have the balls to do it themselves.

†*The owners of the Coq d'Or, the most derelict of the grand old restaurants to survive the swinging sixties, were by 1976 anxious to rid themselves of it. Though the lease was cheap, the sum was by Peter's standards a great deal of money, and as he had not recovered from his unwitting investment in Jean-Marc Moussis' 30,000 bottles of sweet white wine, he was compelled to find partners to support his ambitious project to convert the red velvet leviathan into a bright brash brasserie. He first proposed partnership to two brothers whose business was importing caviare, and for some time toyed with the idea of having in*

the Brasserie the most splendid caviare bar in western Europe – there was a note of caution in this ambition, for he thought it possible that an even more splendid bar might be found in Odessa, a baroque survival from the days of the last Czars. Negotiation with the brothers advanced as far as dining together in the Ritz, but there Peter became aggressively drunk, told them that they knew nothing about champagne, and threatened to thump one of them. Their prompt withdrawal from all arrangements with him at a time when Peter was irrevocably committed to the purchase of the lease compelled him to find other partners in great haste. Michael Caine, who dined occasionally at Odin's, was enthusiastic in his willingness to join him, and the second partner, who joined a year or so later, was Richard Shepherd, a chef trained by Trompetto at the Savoy who, at the age of thirty-two, could be seduced from his employment at the celebrated restaurant of the Capital Hotel in Basil Street into striking out on his own account. Peter took little more than six months to impose his 'Langan look' on the premises, and within another six months of its opening in September 1976, the Brasserie had become essential to the giddier elements of London society.

Everyone wished me luck two meant it Beth Coventry who helped me open it and Pierre Martin of La Croisette "Go ahead," he said "Bring Paris to London". what I wanted was a chic version of the old Lyons Corner Houses and Bertorelli's. I succeeded, helped along the road by Philip Norman's write up in The Sunday Times, it was a most compelling article he wrote about my dream, curiosity if nothing else had the customers knocking the door in metaphoricly speaking of course

The food was either fantastic or bad, the service was best described by Peter Cook in The Daily Mail he suggested that Michael Caine should stick to movies, and that Basil Faulty could give me expert advice.

Here again is the story of theft bailiffs at the door; I used to go in by the back door to avoid the customers and find out the lie of the land before facing a room full of sozzled dissatisfied customers. One customer summed it up "I'm a pensioner as of tomorrow, could I please have my

Bob Marchant: The Glyndebourne Banquet, *1975. On 21 June 1975 Peter gave a banquet at Glyndebourne to celebrate David Hockney's sets and costumes for* The Rake's Progress. *The photographer Bob Marchant later reworked his material into this mock-primitive painting, bought for the Brasserie by Richard Shepherd as a sentimental gesture. The dominating group among the figures comprises David, his friend Henry Gledzahler, and Peter.*

Peter Langans feast for David Hockney at Glyndebourne to celebrate the first night of "The Rakes Progress."

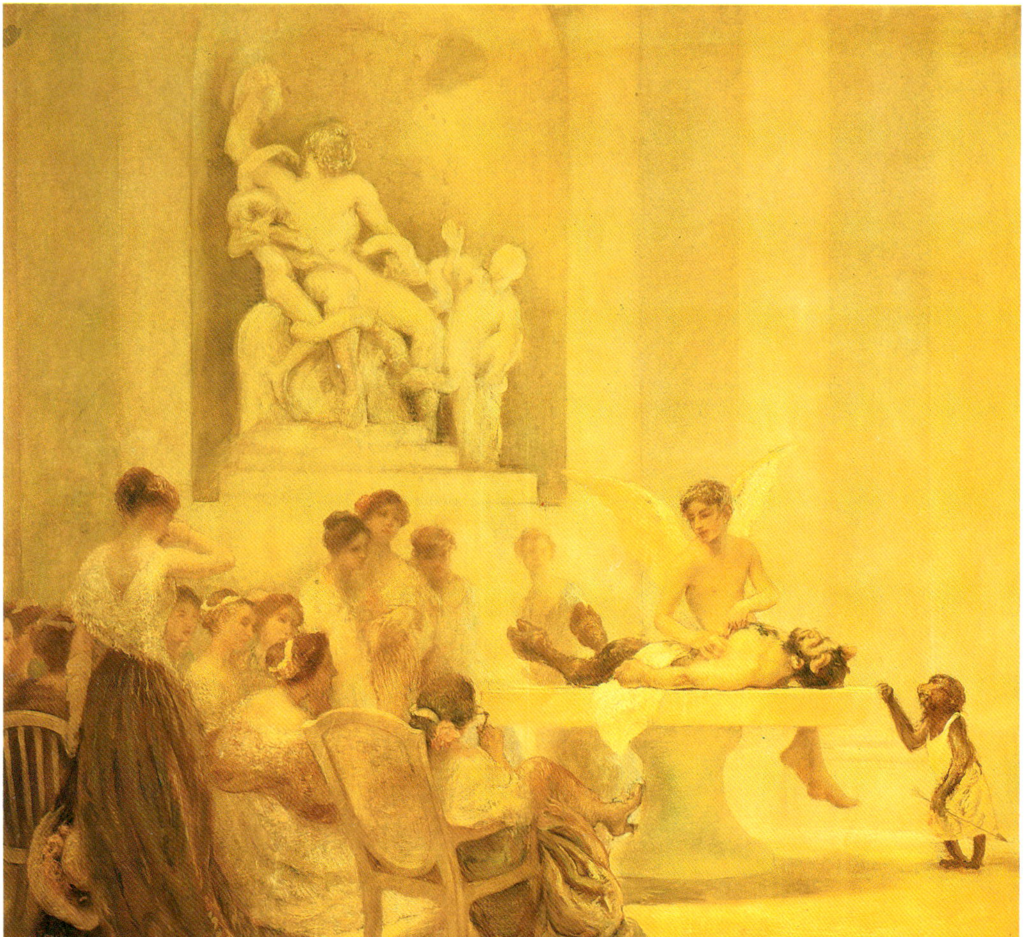

main dish before then"?, it was lunchtime.

This will be a decade of Langans Brasserie which it seems is acknowledged as the United Kingdom's most popular restaurant.

There have been many mad moments, rows fires and strange moments. Michael Caine and Richard Shepherd are straight and reliable – myself, I change with the wind and shift with the breeze. There will be 30 recipes some plain some exotic.

The beginning was madness – theft, a lunatic genius of a chef.
The hiring of Andrew "hatchet man" Leeman to save the floor and Richard Shepherd from the Capital Hotel, to save the kitchen and the business. This was my revenge on David Levin, the proprietor of that hotel.
The slow climb to a reliable watering hold.
Why it is a success.
Stories about the restaurant over the last decade, some quite amusing.
I will have to ask my friends what happened.
Recipes, etc.

†*Once Nigel Dempster had told his tale of Peter's vomiting in the swimming pool of the Cipriani, in Venice, and Angela Levin had it that he vomited on the table in the Brasserie, vomiting hither and yon was established as his party piece and entered the mythology – it is always safe for a journalist to repeat a twice-told tale, but I doubt if any hack ever saw him being sick. He slept on the Brasserie floor often enough, having drunk himself unconscious, and his libido was so lively that there is the ring of truth in his tales of offering limitless champagne to women who might remove their knickers, of licking breasts and biting necks and sitting on their laps – but none who knew that his experience of sex with women began in a broom cupboard exchanging oral pleasantries with deaf and dumb housemaids should find his random sexuality surprising (nor, indeed, flattering). The least amusing of the gossips' tales was that having eaten a cockroach about which a customer complained (surely a variation on the oldest of restaurant jokes), he then threatened to eat the chihuahua nestling in her lap, snatched it from her, and bit it.*

Gaston la Touche: The Anatomy of Love, *circa 1900. In this sumptuous example of* fin-de-siècle *decadence, Cupid, a young satyr and a monkey, all ancient symbols of concupiscence and sensuality, perform a delicately erotic charade for the amusement of the young Parisiennes who were part of La Touche's bourgeois social life.*

Peter liked dogs; he was always thoughtful for mine, and without any hint from me asked that left-overs be wrapped for them, always with something succulent and substantial added to the parcel. I treasure the recollection of his romping in the garden with five very young puppies, his play uninhibited and oral. He had a dog of his own, called Badger (which most of his friends thought a compliment of sorts to Ron Hall, then Editor of The Sunday Times Magazine, *whose nickname it was), a cross-bred sheepdog, marmalade and white, that displayed impeccable manners whenever Susan brought him to Odin's.*

The disgusting and flamboyant Peter promoted by the diarists is more truthfully illustrated in his impetuously filling his arms with daffodils at the stall outside Green Park Underground station – 'I'll pay you later' – and returning to the Brasserie in amiable childish triumph after an early morning squabble over the miserable flowers already there.

CHAPTER 8

Special Days I Remember

In forty years of anybody's life there are special times for all of us – these can be years, months, weeks, hours, minutes or just moments.

My great times have been from the day of my First Communion – I did not realise its significance, but it was a happy day, later the maids at college, my first woman in Sunderland, then meeting a girl in Cardiff, that was the first time I fell in love. The wild early sixties of total promiscuity when half a bitter got you a quick bang in the back of the Ford Cortina.

Special days are also the sad ones when someone you have loved is dead, even when it is expected, it's still a moment of surprise, the tears of relief and sadness – the worst sorrow is when your brain cries and the tears never reach your eyes.

My special times have been all of these emotions, some I don't want to remember, those are the dry tears of darkness and depression.

My trade is eating and drinking so my moments are often memories of good times in the restaurants, where people meet, go home and make love all night, then I feel I have done my job. I suppose that you might describe me as a culinary pimp.

Here also will be the dinners I remember and the special evenings that will never be forgotton.

The recipes here will not be at the end of each chapter, but at the finish on each occasion. There will be Hockney's picnic at Glyndebourne for The Rakes Progress, a Dinner Party at a prostitute's appartment on the Isle St Louis in Paris – a simple supper with a Dukes daughter and her gossip columnist husband in Ham Common and an evening in Venice with Helene Fogarty and her elegant drop out coterie of decaying Friends.

Glynebourne – An evening of excess

Midsummer's day – a story of the evening.
Hockney's favourite night of his life.
The buffet – picnic, the dishes and the recipes.

Dinner with Ginette – a lady of the night.

She works in London and has a superb apartment on
The Isle of St Louis in Paris.
Fellow guests, the food and the wine.
Her taste in food.
The dishes and recipes.

An evening with The Lady Camilla

Her daughter is my god-daughter.
The food is simple and English – i.e. Fluffy Crab Cakes – mustard sauce.
      Roast Stuffed Leg of Lamb.
      Alcoholic Fruit Sponge.

A weekend at Helene Fogarty's house in Venice

Description of the town, the market, the feeling and the dishes and recipes.

CHAPTER 9

My Love for the Grape and the Hop

It is said that the English disease is buggery, the German – flagellation and the Irish – drink, the Irish one probably protected from the other deviations by either a lack of inclination or a horizontaly inebriate condition.

Levity aside, never become an alcoholic like me, the pleasure wanes over the years and suffers a sea change into something wierd and strange, the pleasure becomes a plague. If you like a drink you cannot afford to become an alchie, you either have to give it up, or take a one way ticket to your local cremmy.

Myself, I try to stop all the time, but I often fall by the grapeside. The other morning in that limbo world between deep sleep and wide awake I heard a voice

"Hey Langan can you hear me?"
"What – Yes yes what is it?
"Whose there anyway?"
"It's me I'm your liver"
"So what"
"I'm going on strike, that's so what"

"Bugger off – I've got a hangover"

"Listen Mr Langan, I'm no Arthur SCARGILL. If I go on strike you go to the charcoal grill at Golders Green"

"What do you want?"

"Good living conditions and a years SABBATICAL, otherwise the lads – your balls, kidneys, your heart and whats left of your brain pack up work and with us gone you are buggered old son!"

"OK, OK when do I have to start?"

"Right now, understood?"

I awake to the grim reality of alcoholic poisoning and three days of pain. There is no cure for alcoholic poisoning but there is the Langan Elixir which fixes any hangover. Forget about those rubbishy pseudo cures you see hanging on straps in pubs, this is the definitive cure but only one glass is to be consumed with two of the apricots.

DIRECTIONS: Place dried apricots in the bottom of a jam jar or Kilner jar to twenty five percent of its capacity. Fill the jar with an amontillado style medium sherry, leave for a week the apricots will swell into round rich sodden beauties. The sherry takes the flavour of the fruit. In a week the nectar is ready, it is advisable to turn the jar upside down occasionally, this way each apricot gets to full bloom.

Make as much as you like, the alcohol means that it does not have to be refrigerated but for the morning after, drunk straight from the fridge, this mixture sets you up for the day. It is addictive and as the notice says on a cigarette pack, it can be dangerous to your health.

The apricots with a little of the nectar and vanilla ice cream with slivered toasted almonds make a superb instant desert.

NOTES: There will be a bakers dozen of my own cocktails and two non alcoholic Fruit cups for the younger generation and the poor unfortunates who are on the wagon. Great home made wines can be made in the UK. There will be several recipes. For wines and illicit distilling has a flavour all its own.

†*This recipe is not Peter's; he took it from Nicholas Vilag, Hungarian art dealer, whose invention it was.*

CHAPTER
10

America

A DECADE OF DEBACLE

*N*OTES ONLY It began as a dream and gradually degenerated into a nightmare. Nearly ten years ago I came to California to escape the English winters. Now nine years later I know the loneliness of failure in the cold California sun.

For the first time, I have found out what its like to lose. At this time no Langans Brasserie has opened, Langan has had to suffer the sour odour of failure, for the last nine years I have been a jockey without a ride.

Los Angeles† is a village and it pays to be mister nice guy. In England I'm regarded as a mildly inebriate eccentric, over here they believe me to be a wild British dog, well this Irish, slugger is going to surprise them. It looks like I am finally going to get a ticket to ride.

†*The Los Angeles restaurant almost broke Peter's partnership with Michael Caine, whom he expected to produce enthusiastic wealthy investors by the dozen; when the grand old men of Hollywood failed to respond to his prospectus, Peter became sullen and abusive, and to one of his producers sent a telegram with the legend 'Fuck you Shithead. I do my job better than you do yours.' This tale too has entered the mythology – Peter told it of any wealthy American for whom he did not care, and*

many, not so wealthy, now tell it of themselves.

I have acquired a premises at Century City that will be the largest public restaurant in Los Angeles. it will seat 350 people in one room. My name is already over the door, I want to let the bastards know the Mick is back in town.

This chapter will be about the city of the angels that fell from grace, even a seasoned hustler can be ripped off here, even my friends at the banks have robbed me and the Hollywood promise "Trust me" is apt.

I have been pilloried a few times in *The Los Angeles Times* for describing L.A in Harpers "as a cow with a bad case of the runs – the shit is spread all over the place".

You meet some of the best and most of the worst people in the world over here. Beverly Hills reeks of expensive perfume and ambitious insecurity. Why do I want it? I'm damned if I will be beaten, there is still that arrogance of eventual victory in me, a twenty five year old mentality in a middle aged body.

I will conquer this land of murder, rape, pillage and loneliness by the time this book is written I will have won the restaurant is due to open in March 1988.

This will tell the story of an ageing fox surviving in a social desert.

There have been some good times and there are great american cooks. Home cooking seems to be of a higher standard here, it is however impossible to judge America accurately, each state is like a separate country, I have found it impossible to feel part of a community.

The one thing that binds America together is the fear of a red sharing the wife's bed – I hope I can change but I have been mugged too often.

This is a town where understanding is a disposable tissue and they sell Real Estate on television in six foot plots.

There will be about twenty five recipes in this section. The narrative will be mostly satirical rancid conversation. My letter from america will not be like Alaister Cook's, a producer said to me the other day at a film preview "Peter treat your enemies and friends the same that way you will be safe", well I guess he is a regular guy in this centrefold society with beer jug brains.

CHAPTER 11

England Today and My Favourite Hiding Places

I have been in England for nearly thirty years for most of those years I have been the proprietor of my own business.

Here I will talk about the great restaurants of the U.K. and why they can contribute little to the improvement of the general standards of eating in our country. Restaurants in the country are still middle class and elitist. My opinions of chefs their cook books and the writers on food who have made an impact on all our lives and not just the Harrodites of Knightsbridge and Belgravia.

There are not that many great establishments still operating who were in business when I first arrived. The story of the dead restaurants and the reason why some will survive forever.

There will be my own selection of restaurants† with dishes that can be made at home with ingredients available throughout the country.

Approximately forty recipes.

COOKING IN A FEW MINUTES

Todays world dictates for many a short time to cook. I believe that careful stocking of long life staple ingredients can eliminate the necessity of resorting to packet food. I will show that dinner parties for six can be dished up from three to ten minutes maximum time provided some thought and planning are made in advance. There will be ideas and twenty recipes.

†*Peter's draft of an article for the* Evening Standard *(published on Tuesday 22 September 1987), reproduced below, may give something of the intended flavour of this chapter.*

The advantage of being a guest critic is that there is no need to be investigative about restaurants as your regular columnist does.

My choice reflects twenty-five years of London dining out. In racing parlance I have chosen stayers, Grand National horses who have or will last the course.

This week the column is divided into two sections, first my opinion of Food Guides, second my thoughts on a few of my favourite restaurants.

CRITICS AND FOOD GUIDES

The great ones have been Egon Ronay for his eponymous guide, Raymond Postgate for the Good Food Guide, Quentin Crewe for Harpers Queen in the 60's and Fay Maschler for the Standard's column for over a decade and her own guide to Eating Out in London.

There have been failures like the famous Gault Millau Guide. They were so crass they even put one restaurant in twice under different names and returned to France with muck on their mush.

I remember jolly old Sammy Lohan (Evening Standard) ex-MI5 or something like that – in conversation he always mixed up monosodium glutamate and bromide – and Larry Adler (Harpers Queen). After reading his column, one knew all about Larry and sod all about the restaurant.

The Fay Maschler Guide £5.95 is generally acknowledged to be the best guide to London to date.

The Michelin Guide £1.85 is only useful to Foodophiles who wish to check on restaurants with rosettes. There are only seventeen in the London area. It's as interesting to read as the telephone directory. Loyd Grossman Harpers Queen Guide £6.95 lists 100 London restaurants.

The others – The Good Food Guide £9.95, Egon Ronay Guide £9.95, Ackerman Guide £9.95, A.A. Guide £9.95 are all nationwide and the former two are essential to the traveller.

One final comment – all guides are out of date by the time they are published. Newspaper columns have the advantage of being a week old at the most.

THE RESTAURANTS

GREEN'S RESTAURANT AND BAR

This is the Establishment restaurant of London. The Royal Family have been; Princess Margaret and Sarah of York are regulars.

High Society is drawn here by the charm of Simon Parker-Bowles, an old Etonian, ex-Guards Officer.

They stay because of Beth Coventry's cooking which is simple and very good.

It can be described as either superb English cooking or nursery food, though I was never given lobster, crab or smoked salmon sandwiches when I was a brat. You can dine in the bar during licensing hours on oysters, quails eggs, smoked turkey etc. at reasonable costs.

The room is relaxing, and the staff are good with children, who eat for half price at Sunday Luncheon. Where Wilton's was, Green's is.

THE WHITE TOWER

John and Eileen Stais founded it over fifty years ago and for me this is London's greatest restaurant.

My first visit was in 1959. A gruff friendly voice greeted me and sat me down in the bar of a restaurant that is still a Valhalla of luxury to me. No fey interior designer could ever create a facsimile of the natural spirit of this place.

That night John chose my dinner from the large menu – the two Patés, that is Taramasalata and Paté Diana with Olives and hot toast, then the Fish Salad, followed by Roast Duck stuffed with Bougourie and for dessert – Fresh Mango with home-made Yogourt. I have had the same meal there for nearly twenty-five years.

It is an old-fashioned restaurant with an Establishment clientele. John has passed away by his spirit lives on in Eileen, Mary and family and, of course, in George Metaxas.

LA FAMIGLIA

This old favourite of mine is a family restaurant. The proprietor, Alvaro, has been one of the strong men of the London restaurant trade for over thirty years. This is a fine example of how to keep simple Italian cooking fresh. He still never misses a service.

Londoners who don't read guide books but do know their food, are regulars. His is a chic clientele.

We are lucky to have him here. When he was a child in Rome, Keppler, the Nazi, had him in an execution line-up, with one in ten to be shot. He was lucky, and as he says – "Now every day is a gift from God".

THE BOMBAY BRASSERIE

This is the best Indian Restaurant in London and also the most expensive, but worth it. The food is superb.

It moves in a different world of sophistication and elegance to any other Indian establishment and ranks among one of the best restaurants in the country of any cuisine.

It has a multi-regional menu with food from Goa and the Punjab, Parsi cooking, excellent Tandoori dishes and the outstanding vegetarian dishes which I love best. I often don't get past a selection of starters.

There is a very comfortable bar in which to peruse the long menu.

SIMPLY NICO

Nico Ladenis is probably the best Greek French chef in the world. He has had two other businesses and I hope he has found his niche here.

The culinary Establishment loathe him for his arrogance. He moved back to London again because the people of the suburbs didn't appreciate his self-proclaimed genius.

This place is full for luncheon and dinner. Book in advance or else book for 10.30 in the evening.

He is quite amusing and his food is excellent – as it should be at his prices. It's better to be someone else's guest!

LE SUQUET

This is part of France. The Plateau de Fruit de Mer, brought to London by proprietor Pierre Martin, has no equal outside his other restaurants. Here you don't have to close your eyes to think you are in France; it's where the French in London eat. Martin has more style in his left boot than most of his fellow French patrons put together. Le Suquet is for those who make eating out a way of life.

FOOD FAX

Green's Restaurant and Bar
36 Duke St, St James, SW1 930–4566
Cuisine:	Old fashioned English
Atmosphere:	Chic, chic, clubby, friendly, relaxed
Service:	Excellent
Recommended:	The bloody lot
Price:	£45 for two with modest bottle of wine. Service not on bill. Bar price: best crab/smoked salmon sandwiches £5. Wine by the glass
Credit cards:	All major credit cards
Hours:	Mon-Sat 11.30-1.30 and 6.30-10.45. Sun lunch 11.30-3.30. Bar: 11.30-2.30. 5.30 onwards

White Tower Restaurant
1 Percy St, W1 636–8141
Cuisine:	Refined Greek
Atmosphere:	Old fashioned, charming, comfortable
Service:	The best in town
Recommended:	The roast duck
Price:	£45 for two with Othello wine. Service not on bill
Credit cards:	All major cards
Hours:	Mon-Fri 12.30-2.30 and 6.30-10.15

La Famiglia
7 Langton St, SW10 351-0761
Cuisine:	Italian
Atmosphere:	Family, relaxed
Service:	Good, excitable. Italy wins the world cup every day
Recommended:	Trufolette (home made pasta dumplings)
Price:	£32 for two. House wine £5.35. Service not on bill
Credit cards:	All major credit cards
Hours:	7 days a week 12.00-12.45 and 7.00-11.45

Simply Nico
48A Rochester Row, SW1 630-8061
Cuisine:	French modern high cuisine
Atmosphere:	Comfortable
Service:	Good, professional
Recommended:	Fois gras chaud en salade – apple tart
Price:	£60 for two with wine luncheon. £84 for dinner
Hours:	Mon-Fri 12.00-2.00 and 7.00-11.00

Bombay Brasserie, Baileys Hotel
Courtfield Close, Courtfield Rd, SW7 370-4040
Cuisine:	Indian – Bombay cosmopolitan
Atmosphere:	Sophisticated, elegant
Service:	Good management, very good indeed
Recommended:	Vegetarian dishes – Sev batata puri
Price:	£45 for two with wine. 12½% service charge
Credit cards:	All major cards
Hours:	7 days a week 12.30-2.30 buffet lunch only and 7.00-12.00

Le Suquet
104 Draycott Avenue, SW3 581-1785
Cuisine:	Fish restaurant, French cooking
Service:	Very Parisian
Atmosphere:	You open the door and cross the Channel
Recommended:	Plateau de fruit de mer. Baked seabass
Price:	£50-£60 for two. No service on bill
Credit cards:	All major cards
Hours:	7 days 12.30-2.30 and 7.30-12.00

CHAPTER 12

My Funeral Feast

---

*N*OTES ONLY This has been the diary of an atheist who has at this time no intention of writing about food again. Eating and imbibing has been my life. The Brasserie will be closed for one day of excess

There will be none of the remnants of my family at the wake, boozy carousers bent on a good time. I might decide to have it on my fiftieth birthday – I rather fancy the idea of getting maggoty at my own wake, if I have crossed the bar then the notes below will apply.

FUNERAL FEAST

To be held on the anniversary of my birth, the 13th of May, following my death. Introduction preamble about my likes, dislikes of life in general and some people in particular.

I will have vengeance if I have a slow healthy lingering death. Six members of the human race may get charcoaled before myself.

One Greek Orthodox, three Jewish gentlemen, one Church of England and last, but not least, an American Mormon – this levity to continue, then the dishes for two separate feasts.

First One: is for the Killing Trade.
Recipes and dishes.
Second One: An Sionnac Glic.
Recipes and dishes.

Peter Langan

BRIAN SEWELL

In the early sixties, when all self-respecting art dealers had premises within sight of the line that runs from Sotheby's to Christie's, the Bond Street axis, Nicholas Vilag opened his gallery far away at 25 Devonshire Street in Marylebone. He called it the Fine Art Gallery, but its nature was that of a junk shop, hung to the ceiling with pictures, racked and stacked with unframed prints and drawings, most of them wrapped in polythene, the clinging dirt obscuring their lack of quality and filthying the hands of prying visitors; downstairs, where visitors were not allowed, the basement store was a dark, impenetrable confusion of frames, canvases and bulky folders labelled *London*, *Paris*, *Prague*, *Fruit and Flowers*, or *Erotica*.

Nicholas was an Hungarian Jew whose career as a photographer for *Picture Post* had been interrupted by Horthy and Hitler, and finally broken by internment in England. After the war he began to scratch a living by buying and selling topographical prints, and willy-nilly became an art dealer of sorts; by the time that he opened his shop he had under his wing a number of women who turned penny plain into tuppence coloured, tinting back to life any watercolour that had seen too much sun, and making gay with gouache any simple outline print of

Amsterdam or Dresden. It was with difficulty that I once persuaded him not to colour a fine and very valuable Canaletto etching of Padua. He had a friend, a Royal Academician fallen on hard times, who added signatures to oil paintings or replaced those that were unsuitable; almost every spottily painted modern-seeming picture became a Lucien Pissarro, and many minor English works were made to appear more important with French names that from time to time were changed, for if a landscape failed to find a buyer as a Chabry, the Academician would collect it and return it upgraded to Chintreuil. These signatures were rarely ambitious, for Nicholas had been alarmed when the buyer of a would-be Sisley from his window had at once taken it to Christie's, returning an hour later crestfallen and furious; all were culled from the dictionaries of signatures and monograms that were his only books of reference, and those that he cunningly pressed upon his customers when they asked for confirmation that signatures were authentic.

Nicholas held occasional luncheon parties in Odin's, the unpretentious little restaurant next door, where no one minded that he was a vegetarian, and an omelette could be had for half a crown. It was run by a young man and his wife, James and Kirsten Benson, who cooked, waited and were friendly and occasionally inefficient. One morning in 1966 an accident killed the young man, and Peter Langan, who lodged nearby and had taken to dropping in for breakfast, found Kirsten in tears and incapable of opening the restaurant. He rolled up his sleeves, set to work on the day's menu, and saw that all was ready for those who regularly depended on the restaurant for lunch. With that impulsive act of compassion, Odin's was within weeks transformed in looks, atmosphere, food, wine and price, and became a place to which it was well worth going out of one's way to eat, with Peter taking his first steps as the eccentric cook who wandered among the tables in a bloody apron carrying a meat cleaver, while Kirsten slaved in the kitchen, waiting for late last orders.

The immediately visible transformation of Odin's depended on two things – good crisp white linen on the tables, and pictures on the walls. In time, Peter was to employ the conventional device of waiters who combined quiet efficiency with good looks and an air of sexual ambivalence, under the control of the woman who could be as firm as a governess and as gentle as a mother and who was to become his wife – Susan Langan. Anxious to supplement the meagre income earned skivvying at the *Observer*, in 1967 she answered an advertisement in the *Evening Standard* and became Peter's part-time waitress, but with natural authority and abundant warmth she took charge of the public face of the restaurant, releasing Peter to develop his roles as cook and character.

Peter's first pictures were fine strong watercolours by Patrick Procktor, who lived in the rooms above Kirsten Benson's flat and who came often to the restaurant, and doubtful treasures from Nicholas Vilag's stock. He was equally happy with both, but when he asked me what I thought of them, I could not dissemble and said what had to be said about his purchases from Nicholas. Indrawn breath and muttered obscenities of a kind that I had not heard since my years in the Army were his response. Some days later he returned one of the pictures to Nicholas with the excuse that a knowledgeable client had doubted its authenticity, was charmed by Nicholas's immediate willingness to take it back, and exchanged it for another picture that was twice the price, and on which the signature was just as false. In spite of all this, he continued to buy pictures from the gallery, and occasionally asked me to choose something for him that was 'not too much of a dud'; Nicholas, he argued, held the key of Odin's and accepted early deliveries of food and drink every day, and Peter had no other means of rewarding this help, offered in friendship and with absolute reliability.

When Odin's rose too far in status and in price, Nicholas no longer entertained there, but began to invite what he called his 'Hungarian Mafia' into the small room at the back of his gallery. Here he had installed a decrepit Baby Belling on which he brewed and constantly replenished the non-stop goulash with which he plied George Mikes, author of *How to be an Alien* and *How to be Decadent*, Miklos Rajnai, Director of the Castle Museum in Norwich, and assorted middle-European counts and princelings who earned their livings on the fringe of the art market, while he himself nibbled Cheddar cheese and slightly rotting grapes given away as bird food by the local greengrocer. For pudding he devised two more everlasting dishes, kept in huge sweet-jars, into which fresh ingredients were stirred whenever the levels fell too low for his sense of security – Chocolat Nicholas and Apricots Vilag. Peter claimed the recipe of Apricots Vilag as his own – a not unreasonable theft when all the false signatures are taken into account – but the dish was often on the menu of the first Odin's under Nicholas's name. Chocolat Nicholas was too close to Mrs Langan's Chocolate Pudding (a delicious, rich, soggy, sticky and filling confection devised by Peter's mother, eaten with cream) to appear on the Odin's menu, but it would be a pity if the recipe were lost, for it was uniquely sickening: it consisted only of grated bitter chocolate and chopped almonds stirred into as much clear honey and cheap Cypriot sherry as would give the mixture the consistency of gritty mud; the matured and settled sludge at the bottom of the jar developed a fizzy alcoholic aura of its own, far more intoxicating than the fresh additions. Until the Brasserie opened in 1976, Peter habitually dropped in on these gatherings, tasted everything, made helpful comments on the condition of the various mixtures, and gently teased Nicholas with flattery.

Peter's refusal to let rancour over the fakes colour his relationship with Nicholas led to a topsy-turvy trust between them. They were libidinous – Peter openly boastful, speculative, enquiring, Nicholas grunting and secretive – and there were times when one of the amateur watercolourists employed to enliven Nicholas's stock played amateur in another sense, making both of them happy among the frames and parcels in the basement store, though not together. Peter's 'I'm just going next door for a quickie', said in Odin's to anyone who cared to catch the phrase, meant that he would return in ten minutes with a strangely intense expression and a sheen of sweat.

Though Peter not only knew that much of the stock next door had been enhanced, improved, restored and upgraded, but eventually knew too the identities of all who did this work, he never betrayed Nicholas. On many occasions when wealthy doctors from nearby Harley Street came into the gallery with wads of banknotes for which there were no corresponding accounts, he let his presence and reputation as a shrewd collector lend authority to any assertions that Nicholas might make, even to the extent of saying 'It's in the book,' with a knowing tuck of the head, gleeful at the conversion of untaxed Arab cash into yet another fake Pissarro, a Jewish painter, for the benefit of Nicholas, a Jewish dealer. Nicholas in turn, hearing that Peter was in almost devastating financial difficulties with the larger Odin's in 1975, called him into the gallery and offered him a sizeable suitcase packed with banknotes, saying only 'Take it, take it,' and turning away in tears. Peter, who did not take the money, affectionately described him as 'a mugger who played Good Samaritan to his victims'. When Nicholas died, and was through some carelessness cremated to the words of the Church of England service, Peter, however

Peter on the steps of the Brasserie with his partners, Michael Caine and Richard Shepherd.

much he denied any respect for religious observance and belief, was appalled, and yet could not help remarking 'At least the old bugger was consistent – he even went to meet his maker under a false attribution.'

It was in the first Odin's that Peter cut his teeth as cook, connoisseur and character, with the restaurant very much his personal instrument after Kirsten Benson deserted the kitchen in 1968, remaining his partner, but preferring to spend her time caring for her two children. The menu depended on fine fresh ingredients and simple treatment – no better nor more ample dish of liver and bacon was ever served in London, and bubble-and-squeak was rescued from the left-over shelf and turned into a delicacy – though from time to time Peter did exotic things with pork and ginger. He made a rich mushroom paté in a pastry case, always firm and never soggy, and a more conventional hare paté. For this he used only the hind legs, and once a week delivered the rest of the many carcases in a taxi, bloody and gamey, as food for the dogs that governed my life.

The calculated eccentricity for which he became notorious developed from genuine enthusiasm and enquiry; having cooked something with which he was himself delighted (and he tasted everything), he felt compelled to ask the opinion of those who had ordered it, and snatched odd moments to come upstairs without doffing his apron to say 'I'm the cook. Have you enjoyed your meal?' Gravy stains and a ladle provoked a less apprehensive response than bloodstains and a meat cleaver, and Peter quickly realised that his patrons enjoyed being terrorised and that a bloody uniform brought him custom. When I took Gert Schiff, an American professor of art history, to dinner, Peter put on a splendid Guignol performance, and engaged him man-to-man in untrammelled conversation on erotica and pornography – subjects on which Schiff has published his considerable measure of academic expertise – until his eye lit upon two women dining across the aisle within easy hearing, one pretty and in her twenties, the other rather older. 'I bet they're lesbians,' said Peter, and kept on saying it, as though he were in some way challenging himself; 'I bet I could have the young one. I'm going over to them,' – and he did, with his usual question, 'Have you enjoyed your meal?'

'Why do you ask?' countered the younger woman.

'I'm the cook. What did you have?'

'Oh, some kind of shit. Shit with gravy, I think.'

When my old brown bitch, Susie, was recovering from a hysterectomy in 1968, he invited her to dinner, wore a jacket, and ate with her. She sat on the opposite chair confronted by all the panoply of a place-setting, and ate a dish of diced steak, very slowly, savouring each cube, and gazing about her as though she wished to see and be seen. At a neighbouring table four boisterous Australians objected; their complaints began indirectly, with such remarks as 'Jesus! Now we've seen everything,' and grew to a grumble about not paying the bill in such a filthy, unhygienic restaurant. Peter ignored them for some time, and they had no idea that he, dressed as he was, was anyone other than a customer, but at last he could bear it no longer and, without rising from his chair or raising his voice (and taking care not to disturb Susie's poise), he addressed them with 'I own this joint. I don't care a damn about hygiene. I'd rather have this restaurant full of dogs than Australians – as you can see for yourselves, they have better manners.'

From such encounters developed the Peter who asked any woman with a budding moustache or heavy eyebrows, the Pavlovian triggers of his lubricity, 'How's your bush?' The usual responses were disbelief that the question had been asked or expressions of outrage, but one women so addressed, a cheeky young thing cutting a dash on her pay packet from Fortnum's, lifted her skirt for all to see what she had to offer him.

The self-caricature changed with each new restaurant. For the second Odin's Peter adopted the air of a man engaged in a protection racket and wore suits that might have been smart had he slept in them less often; he bought skewbald co-respondent's shoes and joined a golf club; he took a fancy to my old Daimler with its Mulliner coachwork, and outdid me with a battered 4½-litre Bentley bodied by Freestone and Webb that took more than a year and doubled its cost in restoration and, because he insisted on painting it navy blue (never a Bentley colour), even then looked graceless and heavy (the work was completed just in time for the deprivations of the oil crisis in the winter of 1973/74, and the car was sold at a loss during Peter's financial crisis soon after). When he turned the Coq d'Or into Langan's Brasserie, he drove a bright-green Citroën Deux Chevaux and became the man in the white suit and scarlet braces, the trousers drawn high to reveal the ankle and crumple the crutch; in shirt-sleeves he was often to be seen asleep, slumped across *monsieur le patron's* table by the door, deserted by those whom he had asked to lunch or dinner. I often saw him there, nose to nose in violent altercation, face crumpled with rage and the effort of restraining his fists, and reliving his anger for hours after, neither sweet reason nor champagne tempering his foul mood. This, alas, was the Langan of legend and the gossip column, but only he can be blamed for that, for he deliberately courted columnists and *paparazzi* with such skill that none realised that he exploited them for the benefit of the Brasserie, and that he depended on them to maintain it as the meeting-place for the brash and brilliant that London has lacked since the Café Royal fell into desuetude.

The first Odin's was always full, and Peter often walked round it with a tape measure wondering if he could fit in another table or two; the room was too small to be profitable in the style that he maintained, with more waiters than were strictly necessary, more space for patrons, and his time-consuming insistence on cooking nothing until it was ordered and holding nothing frozen in reserve. He extended the evening hours so that clients could have dinner before or after the theatre, and attempted to have every table occupied twice in between, severely testing Susan's diplomatic skills when early arrivals overlapped diners who had become too comfortable with their coffee, for there was nowhere for anyone to sit with an aperitif other than at their tables. Peter longed to expand. I had scrambled round the Haute Savoie in October 1967, and had returned with tales of delicious local wines and the splendid dishes prepared by Père Bise in his hotel in Talloires on the lake south-east of Annecy. Peter went there a year later, with Susan, and for a while Père Bise became his mentor, and for longer, his close friend. I had also told him of a brasserie in Brussels, all white marble, potted palms and elderly waiters, where in the centre well, men played chess and read newspapers all day, while all round, on a low gallery, serious diners munched substantial meals in silence. Peter denied my assertion that the best French food is to be had in Belgium (and had the example of Père Bise to support him), but he was curious enough to go with me to Brussels and test the brasserie (I

OPPOSITE: *Harold Gilman:* The Negro Gardener, *1905. This rare and distinguished work by Gilman, probably painted in America, was one of Peter's most far-sighted acquisitions. When he lent it to the Royal Academy's retrospective exhibition in 1982, the author of the catalogue likened the picture to the work of Velasquez.*
OVERLEAF: *Richard Westall:* Faust and Lilith, *1831. This absurd picture, one of Peter's rare ventures into the field of old masters, was exhibited at the Royal Academy in 1831. It is of some art historical interest as a document of Delacroix's influence in England, and is amongst the earliest of English illustrations to Goethe's* Faust, *which was not translated until 1823. It is perhaps also a distant response to Canova's* Three Graces.

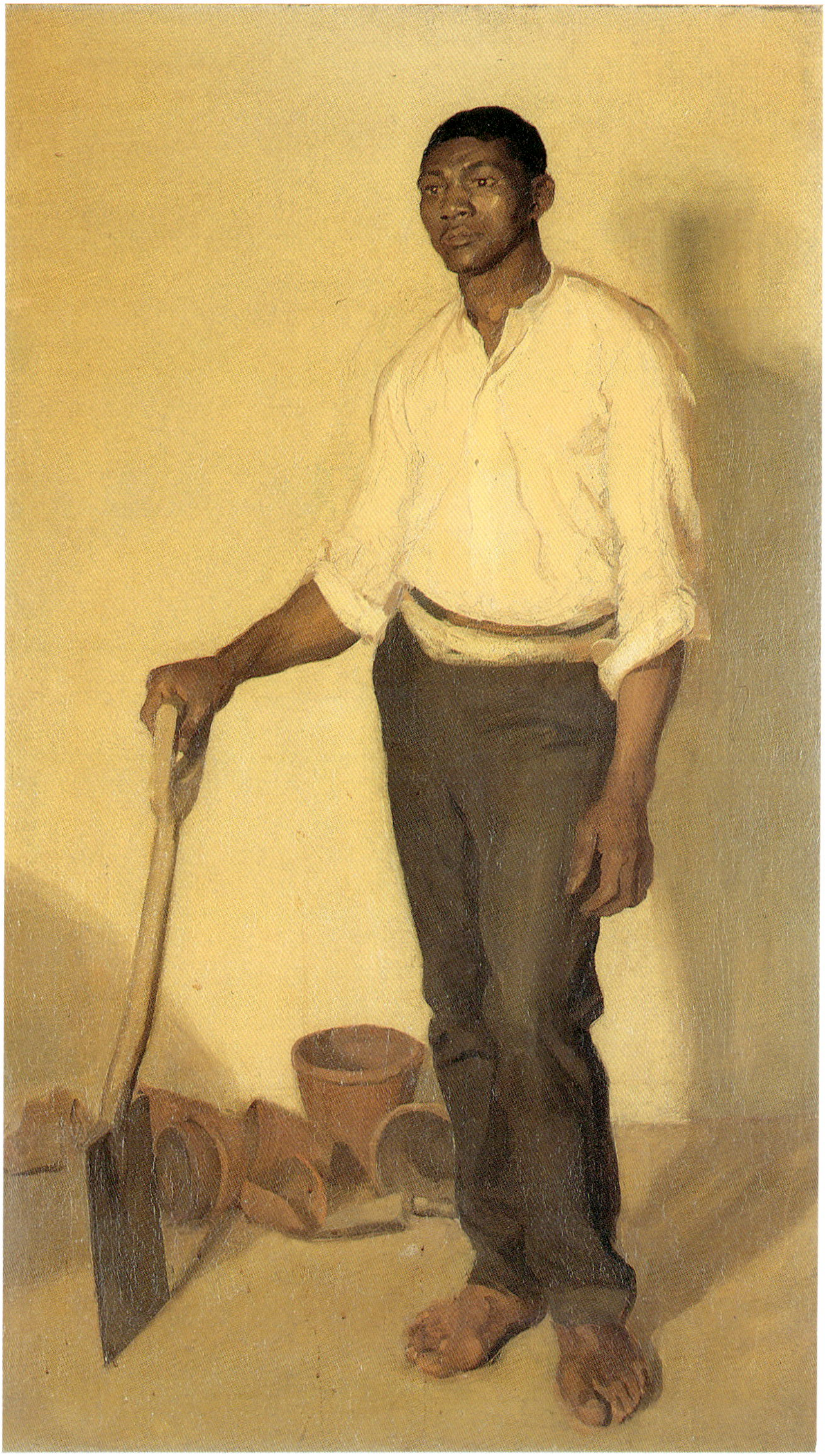

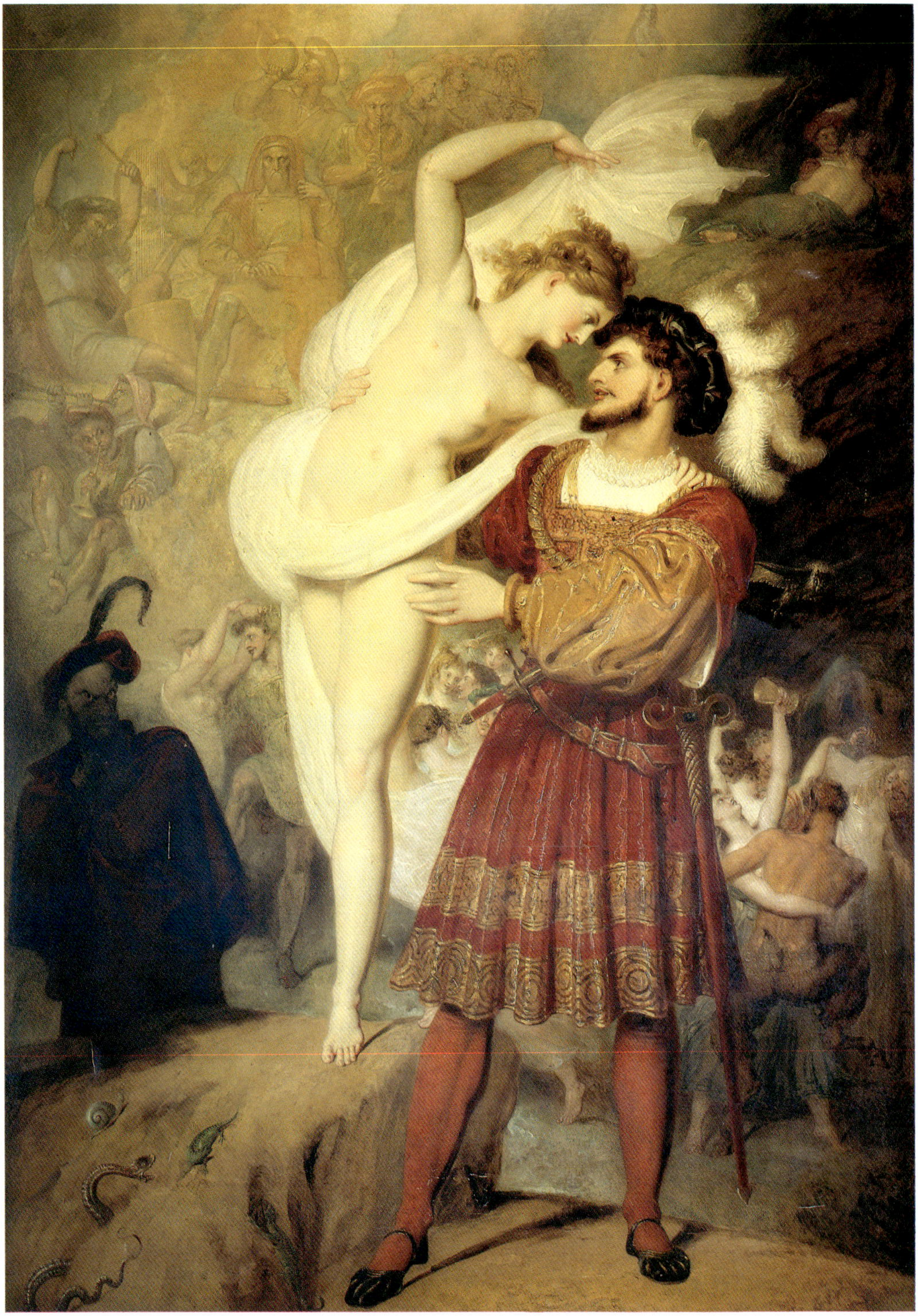

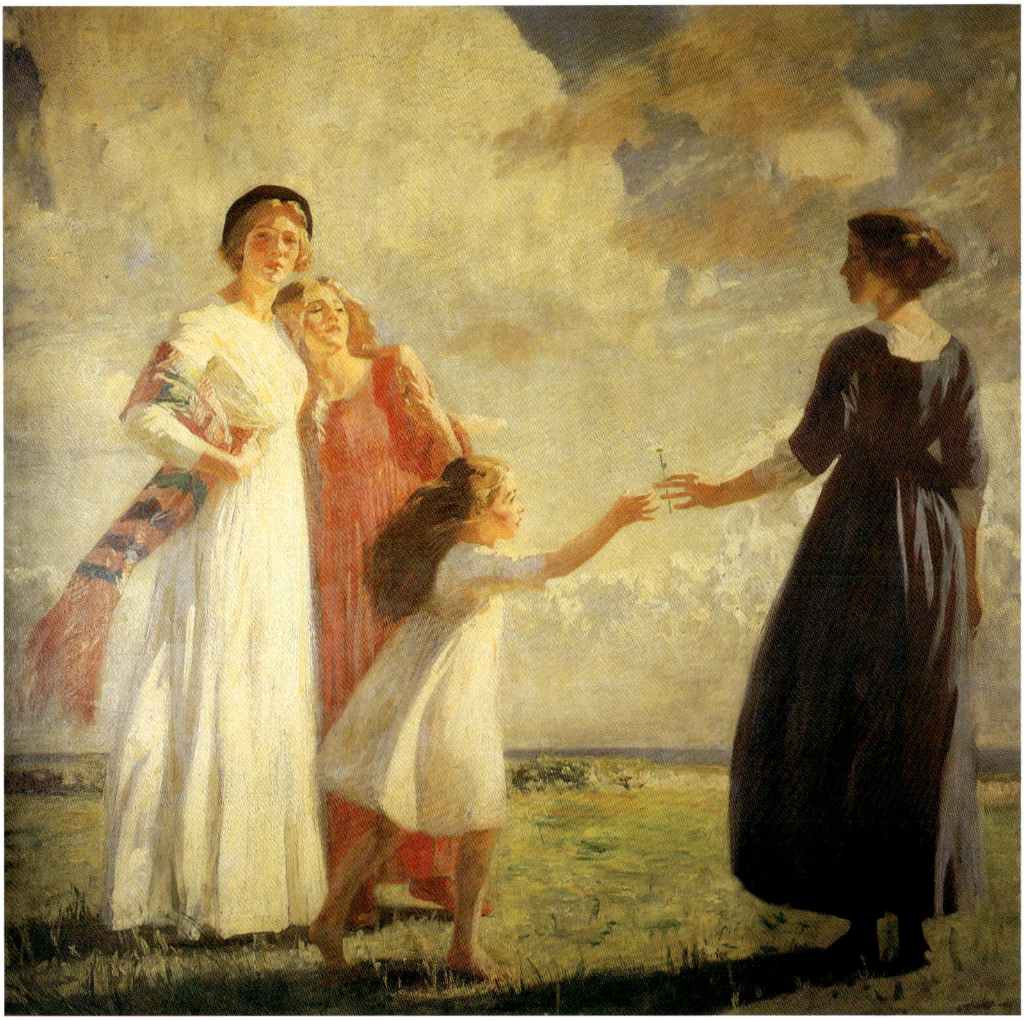

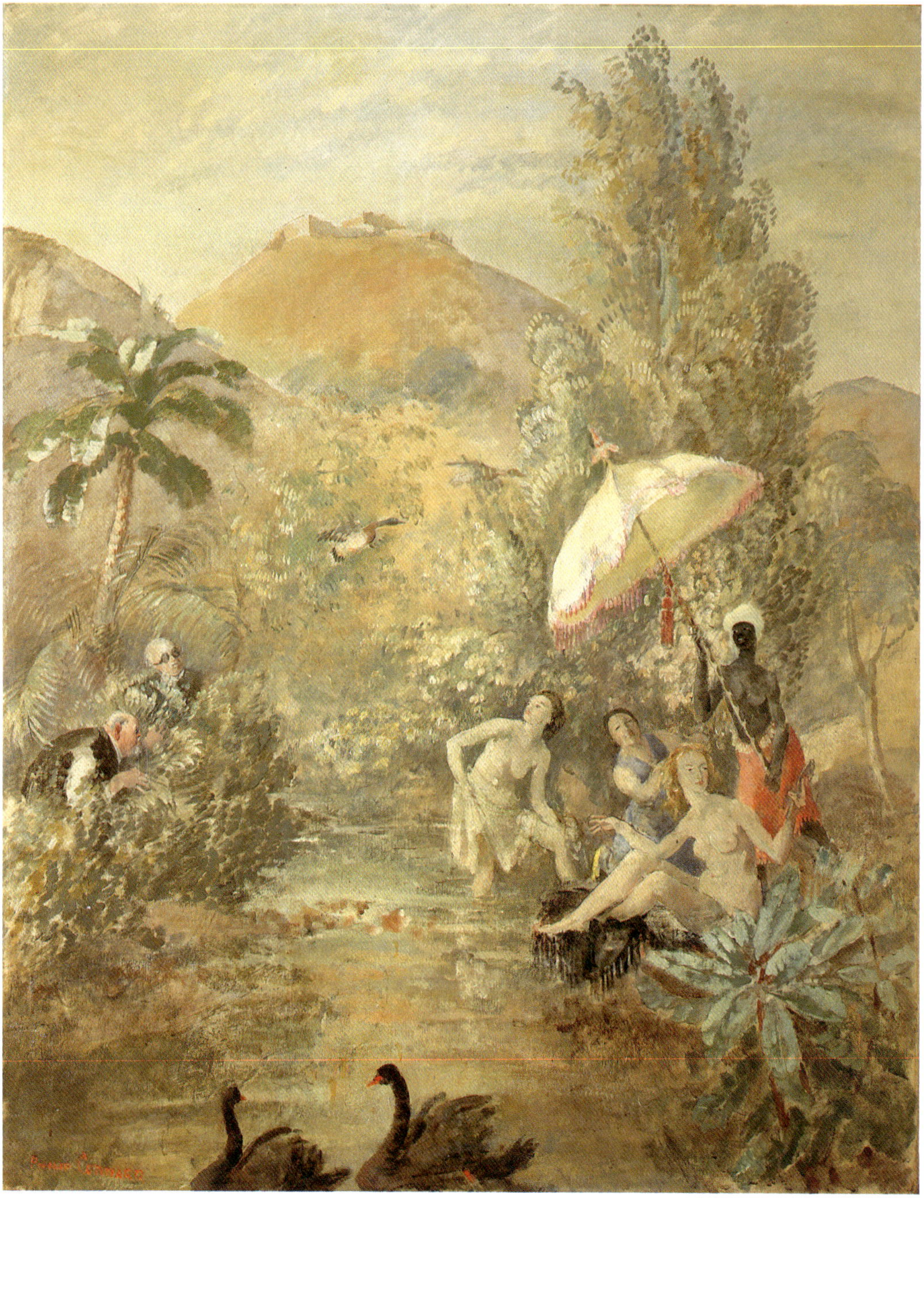

travelled on to an exhibition in Frankfurt the following day and left him to try the flavour of the Belgian whore). Forgetting, or not knowing, how substantial are the demands of the Belgian patron (of restaurants, not whores), he ordered several dishes for both of us and, though astonished by the quality, was appalled by the quantity. *Hors-d'oeuvre riches* the size of a tea-tray and the *Tête de Veau*, a quite recognisable half-head with ear, nostril and eyelashes which no one had even thought of rendering decorously anonymous in the English manner, disgusted him, and he passed most of the food to me to finish after he had prodded and tasted every part of every dish.

I was amused that Peter could use the word 'disgusting' of food and then sample it with such relish, but I learned that he always had two distinct responses – one to the quality of the food and the other, purely visual, to its presentation. Long before *nouvelle cuisine* became high fashion he argued that food should be elegantly and sparingly presented on a larger plate than was customary, so that nothing might be confused with or coloured by its neighbour. Often, eating in Odin's, he called his head waiter (and occasionally the cook), explained exactly what he wanted and asked – sometimes gently and discreetly, but as often in abusive foul temper – that the dish be immediately presented again so as to be sure that they had understood his instructions. Japanese food delighted him not only in its ingredients and parts, but in the delicate isolation in which many of them reached the table.

Within Peter's roly-poly body, and masked by his rumbustious behaviour, lurked a fastidious sensibility and an alert awareness of matters that might trouble no one else. I once saw him enter Odin's, take the vase of flowers from the first table that he passed (much to the surprise of its occupants), sniff not the blooms but the water, and let loose a bellow of rage because it was stale: 'I don't care a bugger if the flowers are dead, only that the water is changed every day – leave them like this overnight and the restaurant will stink like my grandmother's cabbage patch.' In the first Odin's he was constrained by what was

OVERLEAF: *Laura Knight:* The Gift, *circa 1910. Laura Knight rarely worked on so large a scale; here she comes very close to Augustus John's many variations on the theme of* Lyrical Fantasy, *but retains a stronger sense of period identity as well as of portraiture.*
OPPOSITE: *Philip Connard:* Susannah and the Elders, *circa 1934. Connard, with lubricious humour, translated the Apocryphal tale of Jewish virtue triumphant over Babylonian villainy into the worldly thirties by persuading Nancy Cunard to pose as the ancient heroine who refused to commit adultery with the old men in the bushes.*

already there, and by a shortage of money, and made no attempt to remove the open umbrellas that still hang from the ceiling to mask the ugly tracery of conduits and cables, nor to improve the cutlery and crockery; but in the second Odin's, the fastidious Peter with the fine, firm eye of a connoisseur suddenly burgeoned from the experience and frustrations of the first.

In the spring of 1971, Schreiber's, a firm that made fitted wardrobes long before such horrors became fashionable, relinquished their lease at 27 Devonshire Street. These shop premises were next door to the first Odin's, but separated from them by the handsome entrance to Devonshire Court, the block of flats above, and therefore impossible to use as an extension. The overall size of the property, much larger than the first Odin's, was seductive, but it was divided into mean spaces, without any sense of proportion, and all too high. Schreiber's were at first willing to sell their lease to Peter, and then not; they raised the price, and then, just as Peter was on the point of agreement, a string of such senior leaseholders as Freshwater's and Legal and General intervened, and some of the residents of the flats above objected to so radical a change of use for the premises, to yet more cooking smells, noise and rubbish. Only the freeholders, the Estates of Lord Howard de Walden, raised no objection and caused no delay. For a while it seemed that Peter would be frustrated, but I urged him not to lose heart, for at the very same time he was urging me to persevere with the bidding on the house in which I now live, which had reached a ruinous level through gazumping; every time either of us felt inclined to give up, the other painted a picture of the wonderful life that must follow if he did not, and I believe now that it was Peter's determination that bought me my house, and mine that got him his restaurant, each dreaming the other's dreams.

By July 1971 enough of the confusions of leases and landlords had been resolved for Peter to be reasonably sure that he had secured the premises, and I introduced him to Lionel Stirgess, an architect who had long experience in designing restaurants and making the best of bad buildings for clients unwilling to waste money on architecture. The usual conflicts between architect and client followed, with Peter telling Lionel what he wanted to do, and Lionel telling Peter that the building would fall down if he did it. The awkward walls could not be altogether removed, but Lionel gauged where it was safe to break through them, and did what could be done to suggest a continuous flow of space instead of a disjointed series of closed boxes. Peter liked the dark colour scheme at Frederick's in Camden Passage, which Lionel had designed a year or two before, but had so little money to spare for decoration that Lionel had to devise the simplest of schemes to mask the mean and scruffy interior: the ceilings were covered in dark cork tiles, the walls painted cream, and the ugly windows turned into soft fields of light by the simple device of hanging very full fibreglass net curtains from floor to ceiling. Peter introduced the only touch of luxury when he asked Christine Leder (now famous for her picture frames and furniture restoration) to gild with real gold leaf a section of wall near the entrance, where he intended guests to wait in comfort if their tables were not ready; it was an extraordinary but beautiful extravagance, and yet another example of Peter's natural instinct for the rightness of visual effects.

My part in all this was to find pictures – bought, begged, borrowed and to be 'eaten down' – but it was a damnable time of year to be doing it, for Christie's and Sotheby's were about to close for the long summer breaks that they then had until mid-October, and we were at the mercy of dealers. Peter was curious about old masters and suffered the common delusion that any impenetrably dirty wreck would, simply through his buying it, be converted into a masterpiece. He was in danger of falling into the Vilag net again, attracted by the acreage of an eighteenth-century landscape that a hundred years ago had been scoured thin and robbed of detail by a housemaid with a scrubbing brush, and since mercifully obscured by a century of coal fires and nicotine. 'It must be by someone – if only you could find out who,' said Peter.

'Come to lunch,' said Nicholas in his guttural and always audible whisper, 'I have a proposal to make.'

The proposal was that I should give the picture a resounding attribution (Nicholas, flattering me, used the word 'scholarly') in return for a cut of the profit. It was not the first time that he had suggested such a thing, and by no means the last (nor was I the only art historian taxed in this way – he was a constant trouble to the lesser librarians at London University's Witt Library of photographs and reproductions); he simply could not understand that if he had a Michelangelo on his wall I would tell him so without any thought of self-interest, but by the same token I would not engage in any of his Byzantine scheming.

Instead, I diverted Peter into the then unfashionable field of pictures painted by British artists at the turn of the century and on into the 1930s.

It was easily done, for Peter's eye could, with little prompting, perceive the quality, and the prices were easily within his reach; that he could buy a late Sickert a yard long for £300 convinced him that he should, for the moment, concentrate on this field. He was working from four in the morning, when he did his marketing in Covent Garden and the City until after midnight, when last orders were done, and had no time to spare for galleries and art dealers, but one dealer with a suitable stock of pictures ranging from Max Beerbohm to David Bomberg gave me the keys of his gallery so that I could take Peter there on a Sunday.

We had lunch with Susan not far from St James's, in a café that specialised in the luncheon-voucher trade during the week and in misguided tourists on Sunday, and then the three of us walked to the gallery, where I had been carefully instructed on the order in which to open innumerable locks, and on how to turn off the burglar alarms. Dismayed to find the door not locked at all, and the alarm silent, our immediate thought was that we were about to interrupt a burglary. It was, instead, a scene of lechery that we disturbed, of which the first hint was a voluminous pair of gripper-knickers (a hybrid undergarment then much fancied by the ample woman as a comfortable substitute for the roll-on and the lesser corset) at the foot of the tall red velvet chair that normally served as an easel for prize pictures, but which had just been the prop of passion. Shame-faced, yet in some curious way pleased to have been caught in the act, the elderly dealer (who had forgotten giving me his keys) pulled himself together, stroked his mussed hair and talked of Sickert, Conder and Glyn Philpot, while his substantial mistress cowered in his little office, and the rest of us trod warily to avoid the snare of her magenta-flowered knickers.

With very little money Peter established more than the nucleus of a serious collection of what auctioneers and dealers now classify as Modern British art. He was not interested in famous names, and was just as happy with such obscure painters as Alfred Hayward, Graham Robertson and Stephen Spurrier as with Sickert, Sims and Connard – whose mischievous picture of Nancy Cunard posing naked as *Susannah with the Elders* delighted his lubricious humour. He wanted to mix large, impressive pictures with small and pretty things that might help to create an intimate atmosphere peculiar to particular tables, and he wanted all to look as though they had matured into a collection formed over many years, rather than been bought as mere decoration in a hasty trawl

David Hockney: The Restaurateur, *1972. The etched portrait of Peter was issued in an edition of eighty pulls inscribed 'Peter at Odin's'. He holds the umbrella that had become a symbol of the first restaurant's identity; when reproduced as a menu cover, as here, the inscription was omitted.*

through the London art market. Such an aspiration would be impossible to achieve now, for the Modern British market has boomed into the many tens of thousands and the stock is much depleted, but in 1971 it was plentifully stocked with unfashionable pictures, and we were occasionally very lucky, as with almost the last sale of the season at Sotheby's, on the afternoon of Thursday 22 July, when the second stage in the dispersal of Laura Knight's studio took place. In this sale there was an enormous oil painting, seven feet high and eight wide, dating from 1910 or thereabouts, when her work was still fresh, painterly and luminous; it was subjectless, in the same sense as many Augustus Johns of that period are, and reflected his many variations on the theme of *Lyrical Fantasy* – three lush young women, one of whom offers a daisy to a little girl, in a wind-blown Cornish meadow set against the sea. It was filthy dirty, but I was utterly seduced by it, and Peter was persuaded by its measurements, which perfectly fitted the wall on the right of the restaurant's entrance. He bought it for £190, and to put that price into present perspective, Sotheby's sold a kindred composition in 1988 for £78,000.

When the picture was delivered to Odin's it would not go through the door, and there followed a desperate pantomime on the pavement, with Peter uttering disgusting oaths and insults (these last addressed to me), while the rest of us wondered if a window could be removed; in the end, it was put back on the van and set to Peter Newman's studio in Hollywood Road, Chelsea, for hinges to be inserted in the stretcher so that the canvas could be folded. We should have asked him to reline it, but there was neither time nor money, and the picture is still in need of that attention. When at last it was inside Odin's I spent several days cleaning it, a task so Augean that I abandoned all the careful techniques learned at the knee of Stephen Rees-Jones (my old professor at the Courtauld Institute), and descended almost to the level of the housemaid with the scrubbing brush, for the picture had never been varnished, and dirt was deeply ingrained in the unprotected oil paint.

Another stroke of good fortune was finding a large picture by Gaston la Touche, a Frenchman of much the same period as Sickert, to vary the English theme. La Touche was not a great painter, indeed he could be described as an accomplished amateur, but once in a while a minor painter may produce a masterpiece, and this is his. The subject is *The Anatomy of Love*, in which Cupid, an adolescent boy, appears to open the rib-cage of a young bearded satyr and search for his heart, watched by an audience of elegant young women and a monkey; the monkey is a complex symbol, representing both lust (wearing white underclothes to conceal the visible signs of his concupiscence) and art (*Ars simia Naturae* – Art the ape of Nature), and he is the only creature in the audience exhibiting compassion and distress instead of gloating curiosity. When I took Peter to see the picture, the gallery's owner was being berated by a woman who had seen it in the window and had recognised its simmering sensuality; she was literally screaming that it was obscene, and that the dealer had no business to be selling *yellow* pictures as yellow is the colour of lust. Peter played spectator for a few moments and then joined in: 'Don't worry my dear. I've come specially to buy that picture. I *like* a bit of lust.'

In search of very small paintings, I took Peter to see Eliot Hodgkin, whose work I had been collecting for some years. Eliot, a cousin of the then unknown Howard Hodgkin, painted still lives of fruit, flowers, vegetables, feathers, eggs and any object with a quality that could be edged beyond mere realism; his paintings are intensely realistic, and yet unreal, and once seen, they influence the eye of the spectator so that it is impossible for him to see a dead leaf, a shell fallen from a bird's nest or an overblown tulip without something of Eliot's heightened vision. Eliot always quoted two prices, one for payment by cheque, the other, rather lower, for cash. Peter bought four paintings from him with a wad of notes, but I recognised the signs of Eliot's distaste and knew that the visit was not a success, for he had shown us pictures grudgingly and sparingly, and Peter had not been allowed to see or buy the best. Eliot said later that he found it difficult to believe that anyone so boorish could understand or appreciate his work – or any paintings, for that matter – and asked that I should not again bring him to the house. I felt that I had failed them both, for Peter was wise enough to know that he had bought pictures that were not nearly as good as they might have been, while Eliot had felt forced to sell, for my sake, pictures that he would have preferred not to let loose from his studio. I could never persuade him to eat in Odin's, and when he and Peter met in my house over dinner, Eliot said (by no means *sotto voce*), 'I knew I should have asked who else was coming.'

Patrick Procktor was the first of the painter patrons of Odin's; Peter bought from him the large and handsome watercolours that began the change in the first restaurant's character, and Patrick introduced David Hockney and Ron Kitaj, both of whom Peter fed in exchange for pictures, drawings and prints. When he showed me his first Hockney and I questioned the extravagance, he dismissed it with 'That's all right, David's eating it down.' Arranging for artists – and even dealers – to 'eat it down' became Peter's standard way of paying for pictures, and there may well have been evenings at the first Odin's when tables occupied by artists and their friends wiped out all profit.

Peter claimed that his first commission to Patrick was to paint a watercolour portrait of Kirsten's two children in 1968, marking the day on which she left the restaurant in his sole care, but his watercolour of a live black lobster on a Persian rug, used as a menu cover, is inscribed 'For Peter, Kirsten and Odin's' and must have been painted earlier that year, before Kirsten's retirement from the kitchen. The double portrait was later torn in half, and, much later, the halves were discovered and pasted together again by Patrick; it is said that it was the victim of a raging quarrel, but no one now remembers who tore it. I know only of a parallel event in which a painting of Lois Fuller, by W.H. Barribal, that I had given Peter, was savagely knifed by one of the women in his life.

Peter also used as a menu cover Patrick's watercolour portrait of Paul Kasmin, son of John Kasmin (Hockney's celebrated dealer), in which the tousle-haired boy sups a bowl of soup. In 1973 he paid Editions Alecto to print it as an aquatint, *Pea Soup*, but the patch of vivid chromium oxide green within the bowl could never have been achieved even by watercress, let alone by mushy peas. This he gave to friends; mine, the second of fifty impressions, has a spot of real pea soup in the wide margin – a tiresome mischief that Peter found amusing.

Another cover followed – Peter with a glass of wine – and a study of John, a waiter, with Peter at the table, was used for the wine list. The cruellest portrait of Peter is a watercolour of 1974 in which he is slumped and drunk; and by painting him head on, small, and at the bottom of the paper, Patrick made him resemble a drowned mullet. There were other watercolours, but these, it is rumoured, were destroyed when Peter dropped them into a fizzling frying pan.

When searching for large pictures in 1971 Peter acquired from Patrick

Patrick Procktor: Venice, *1979. Peter commissioned Patrick Procktor to paint murals of Venice in the upper room of the Brasserie. Peter hoped for views of the city in winter, but Patrick gave him views in high summer; they quarrelled and Peter vandalised the murals with coats of varnish the colour of tobacco stain. Princess Margaret committed a lesser vandalism with her fingernail.*

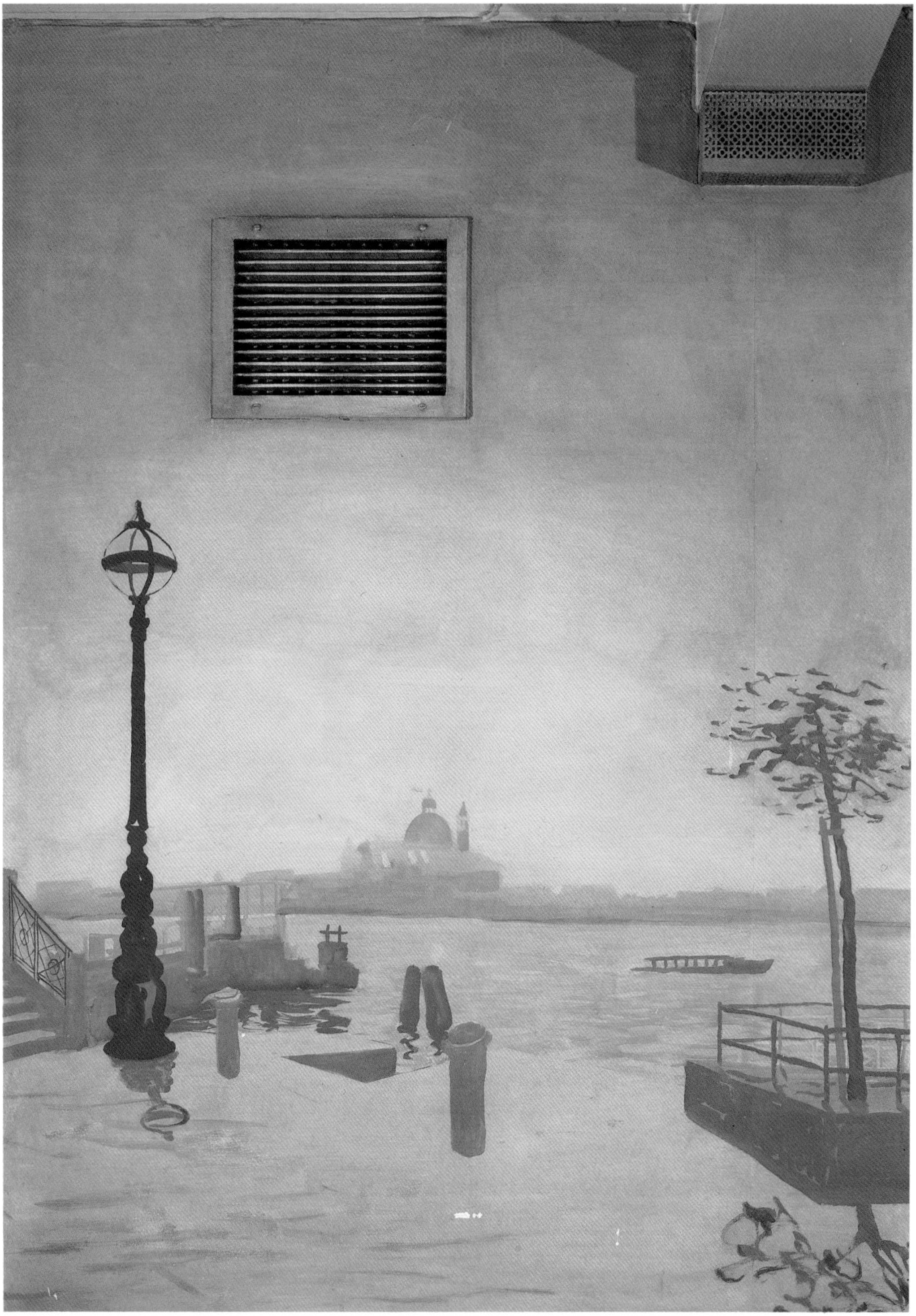

Langans Brasserie – Stratton Street, Piccadilly. Telephone: 01-491 8822

two big, ugly and robust oil paintings of a kind that I had not seen since he first exhibited with the London Group and the Young Contemporaries in the early sixties, when some of us thought that he promised to be a stronger painter than Hockney. This was one of many occasions when I was startled by the courage of Peter's buying and by the breadth of his connoisseurship. He was not in the least deterred that these pictures resembled nothing in Patrick's later work, that they were not even recognisable as Procktors to anyone who had not see the very early exhibitions, and that they had lain unsold and unloved in the studio for the best part of a decade. He saw in them an innate strength and quality, and that was enough to make him want them.

Peter burgeoned as a connoisseur with astonishing speed as he assembled the distinguished and idiosyncratic collection of paintings for which he is now as famous as he is for his restaurants, but he remained wilful and mischievous. Visitors waiting in the reception area of the second Odin's were, and still are, occasionally dismayed by the large drawing inscribed by Ron Kitaj 'for Peter and food', for it is of two men and a woman in the underwear stage of foreplay. Further in, there is another drawing by Kitaj, almost as provocative, and quite inescapable by those who sit at the nearest table; in this, a young naval officer tentatively touches the prominent nipple of a girl who seems not to be his companion, and the melancholy tenderness of the episode is enhanced by an extraordinary softness in the drawing technique. The third of these openly erotic descriptions – rather than evocations – of sexual episodes is even more challenging to the patron of the restaurant, for the image is of a woman in a slack and open pose, ugly and obvious, with, behind her, a younger woman and a man engaged in fellatio.

Peter enjoyed such provocation, for it was part of the openness over sexual matters that coloured so much of his life and so many of his relationships; he took all aberrations in his stride with curiosity and compassion in equal measure, and his amused sympathy for his homosexual friends inclined him, occasionally, to make matches in that field, and be gleeful as he watched developments, whether or not they were successful, though he himself was, as he put it, 'irredeemably heterosexual'. In the last year of his life, distressed by the death from

David Hockney: Peter Langan, Michael Caine and Richard Shepherd, *1976. This drawing, unlike most of the other menu covers (which stand in their own right as works of art), was designed for that purpose for the Brasserie; it is still in use.*

AIDS of so many friends, he became passionately concerned with raising funds for London Lighthouse, Britain's first major residential centre for those afflicted with this plague, and played a crucial role in setting up an auction at Christie's on 2 November 1988. His help was acknowledged in the catalogue with as neat a characterisation as was ever penned: 'Peter Langan has not only charmed, driven and bullied us all as only he can, but also made major donations to the sale.' David Hockney contributed a painting called *Gauguin's Chair*, a bright and charming picture, wayward in perspective, that was the last lot and, with by far the highest bid of the auction, brought it to a spectacular conclusion.

Peter had known David Hockney since 1967 when he was painting the great picture known as *The Room, Manchester Street*, a life-size portrait of Patrick Procktor in his studio that is a thing of extraordinary delicacy and elegance, setting the subject against the light and making his tall willowy body seem translucent; during breaks between sittings Patrick brought him to the first Odin's. David's biographer, Peter Webb, a polytechnic lecturer in art history, is in error when he suggests that they did not meet until 1972 – but then most of his observations on Peter are a cross between an entry in a gossip column and a Chinese whisper: '... Langan had formerly earned his living as a petrol salesman with a big expense account, and found that he enjoyed lunching his customers more than selling them oil. He went into partnership with an architect friend and opened a restaurant called Odin's in London in 1972 which became a great success. Hockney, who loves good food, became a regular patron; he drew Langan standing under an umbrella as an illustration for the menu. When Langan's Bistro opened later in the same year, he drew him in the restuarant for the new menu...'* The truth is that David was often to be seen with his lover, Peter Schlesinger, and other friends at the table right at the back of old Odin's, where half a dozen or more were crushed into space for four, obstructing the entrance to the ladies' lavatory.

The principle of 'eating it down' was established very early on; indeed the first print that I saw for the *Grimm's Fairy Tales* series published in 1969 was a pull of *The Enchantress with the Baby Rapunzel* that David gave Peter before the set was properly for sale, and David himself records a

---

*Peter Webb, *Portrait of David Hockney*, Chatto and Windus, 1988, p. 149.

portrait study of Peter made that same year – though with characteristic disregard for spelling he calls him Peter Langham.*

They became and remained close friends, but I have often wondered whether this would have been the case had they met a little earlier, for David radically changed his style after 1965 and rejected all that was rough and crude, all that depended on a darkening canvas that was bare of paint and priming, in favour of careful finish and a measure of precise and conventional drawing; Peter, I suspect, would not have cared for the deliberately childish style of some of the earlier pictures. His affectionate respect for David as an artist was based entirely on his response to the work that was part of their common experience; it is remarkable that though he was happy to retrieve early pictures by Procktor, he made no attempt to acquire an early work by Hockney and, when I offered to lend him my example of Hockney juvenilia, viewed it with amused distaste.

Hockney served Peter both brilliantly and cruelly, his long series of portraits charting the changes in Peter's face, figure and demeanour with an accuracy that was at first warm towards the vigour and generosity of the man, but at the end verged on the caricatural as Peter drifted into the boastful drunkenness of his last years. David's portrait study of July 1970, a year before the anxieties of the second Odin's began, is a drawing of great beauty and strength; in coloured crayons, it shows Peter with much more dark hair than any of us can now remember ever topping his perspiring brow (and it did perspire), with his tie wayward, and the stripes of his gaudy blazer framing and supporting a figure full of presence. His menu cover portraits of Peter – alone, or with his French wine merchant, or with Michael Caine and Richard Shepherd, his partners in the Brasserie – greatly contributed to the success of all Peter's restaurants and became essential souvenirs for tourists, trophy hunters and those who thought any Hockney memorabilia must sooner or later be of Beatlemania value. (None of the restaurants has kept an archive, and there is now no complete record of David's work for them.)

What was perhaps David's first menu design, dated 1972, shows Peter unshaven and tousle-haired, but with his tie properly knotted, seated on a banquette in the first Odin's, the depth of the restaurant behind him, with the merest outline of Susan and a waiter, and the upturned

---

*Nikos Stangos, *David Hockney by David Hockney*, Thames and Hudson, 1976, p. 194.

umbrellas above. The crayon drawing of Peter with his wine merchant, made in Paris in the summer of 1975, still hangs in the larger Odin's, an observation of beady-eyed competence, slightly mocking and much less warm and sympathetic than the blazer portrait. As time passed, David's portraits became still more mocking and caricatural. One, a small head in oils painted on a copy of *The Times* (a curiously impermanent support for a painting, impossible to preserve in its original condition), showed him pink-flushed and pie-eyed with drink, his mouth agape, his tie pulled far to one side, and with no sign of his short neck; Peter disliked it so much that he could never bring himself to hang it and gave it away during the summer before his death.

In Los Angeles David painted another, much larger portrait, some five feet tall; on grey paper with a disturbingly heavy grid line, it shows Peter seated at a table with a glass of red wine, the red flush of his face heightened by the green of his shirt and the surrounding green shadows, his expression set in an obstinate glower. Though in oils, the run of the paint is so free that the portrait has the character of a large crayon drawing, leaving most of the paper bare; apart from the detailed portrait element of the small head, David was much more concerned with painting a picture than a portrait, and it is a skilful exercise in a limited palette of very strong colours, all made vibrant by the cold grey ground of the paper. To some of Peter's friends this picture is known as *The Byron Portrait.* He loathed the expensive silver frame in which David gave it to him, and had to be restrained from replacing it with one of natural timber; he seems not to have realised that the glister was essential to such vibrant colour.

The least appealing of David's works given to Peter in exchange for food were not portraits, but a still life of flowers in a vase with a brilliant red lobster, set against a black ground, and a view of the interior of the larger Odin's in which he includes an outline of Kitaj's drawing of the sailor and the girl. Both are freely drawn in pastels, almost gaudy; Peter did not like them, but they came to him when David's work was changing and, in experimental mood, he was making one of his many attempts to escape from the tight, almost academic drawing style that he occasionally felt was a restraint on his expression and development. Flowers carefully drawn and realistically painted had occasionally played a significant role in his work since 1971; they counterbalance the destabilising curves of the chrome steel chair in the profile portrait of Sir

Peter, photographed by David Bailey.

David Webster of that year, and are central to several other works. The trouble with Peter's two sketches is that neither of them is as disciplined as these finished pictures. In the still life, the black ground sharpens the predominant reds and oranges and denies the flowers any sense of space, light and translucence, the very charcteristics that were fundamental to most of David's work in the seventies.

David's last painting of Peter was a portrait on eight separate small canvases, hardly dry when it was exhibited at the Emmerich Gallery, New York, in October 1984. He painted several of these multiple portraits, including one of himself, in which only odd parts of the head and body, not necessarily in proportion, appear alone on each canvas. They were an extension of the technique developed in the polaroid photograph assemblages, in which parts of the sitter were photographed from different angles and pasted together overlapping so that they formed a kaleidoscopic commentary, but in the paintings each part is single and separate, in much the same way as the Instruments of Passion and the hands and faces of Christ's tormentors are portrayed in Northern Renaissance altarpieces.

I suspect that Peter felt much greater affection for David than David did for Peter, and that David was one of the few men whom he held in awe. Peter, who never dropped names, was nevertheless inclined to boast when he had been to David's studio; but when I went with him to Powis Terrace he behaved as though he were begging alms for charity, and in Pembroke Studios he played wallflower with the latest boyfriend while David and I discussed the difficulties involved in making large-scale changes to a picture in acrylic paint, with the ten foot portrait of George Lawson and Wayne Sleep in transition for the fifth time. Peter was inordinately proud of having provoked David to pose stark naked with Ron Kitaj, and for having taken the photograph of that startling event that was to be used as the cover of *The New Review* in January 1977, in which they argued for a return by other artists to the figurative art for which both were famous among a wearisome host of painters notable for painting pictures that represented nothing. Peter, a spectator at an early stage in the discussion, challenged them to bear witness to their beliefs and protestations with their own nakedness, and it was inevitably not the arguments but this frivolous jape that caught critical attention when the magazine was published.

Peter had a loyal and romantic element in his character, and it was this that led him to claim that his Glyndebourne banquet for David was the most moving and exciting event in his life. In the summer of 1974 David had been commissioned to design sets and costumes for a new production of Stravinsky's *The Rake's Progress* at Glyndebourne, and a year later, at the first performance, on 21 June 1975, Peter celebrated the occasion with a magnificent open-air banquet on a vast long table on the lawn that was a deliberate and ostentatious challenge to the dreary conventional food provided by the Glyndebourne restaurant. Little, however, was consumed in the interval, so anxious were David and his friends, and it was not until the performance was over, and acclaimed a resounding success, that the banquet really began, with stage-hands and technicians joining the cast, the orchestra and David's guests for an impromptu *fête champêtre* that continued far into the night.

The first part of the event was recorded in a mock-primitive picture, now hanging in the Brasserie, to which Peter was so sentimentally attached that he could see no fault in it, though it is one of the few pictures that he himself did not buy. Against a background of rising green hills dotted with piebald cows stands Peter's long table with its display of hams, lobsters, pies and fruit and, in homage to David, a vase of the tulips that so often appear in his paintings; the dominating group among the figures comprises David, his friend and apologist Henry Geldzahler, and Peter, in the white uniform of a chef; in homage both to Hockney's designs and to Hogarth's prints from which they derive, the long inscription identifying the event is in precise and elegant eighteenth-century script. The artist was Bob Marchant, an Australian photographer present at the banquet (whose photographs are reproduced in Webb, *loc. cit.*, where an illustration is wrongly identified as depicting a banquet for the first night of *The Magic Flute* in May 1978); he later returned to Australia and became a much celebrated painter (only there are such things possible). Richard Shepherd bought the picture for the Brasserie as a sentimental gesture.

The second Odin's opened almost two years after its conception, on a Saturday early in 1973. Peter disliked his Saturday clientele, describing them as 'weekend wankers out to please their wives', but Saturday was the night for which the first Odin's always received too many bookings, and on this occasion, for the first time ever, none was refused. His small staff padded with such friends as me and John White (now an art dealer

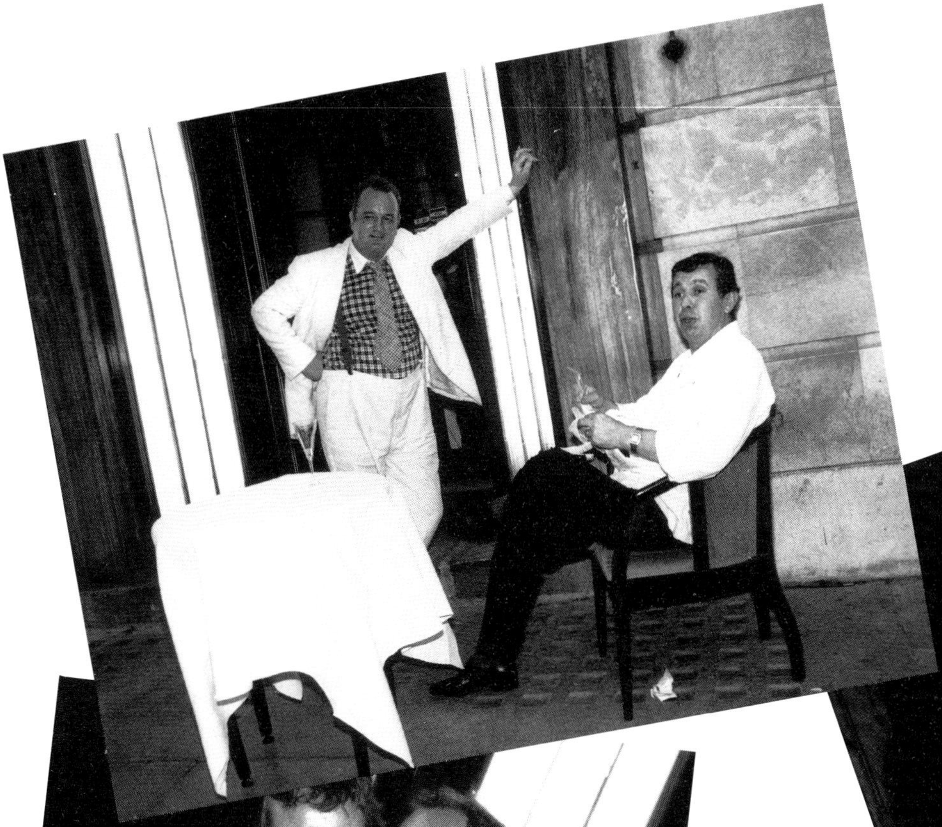

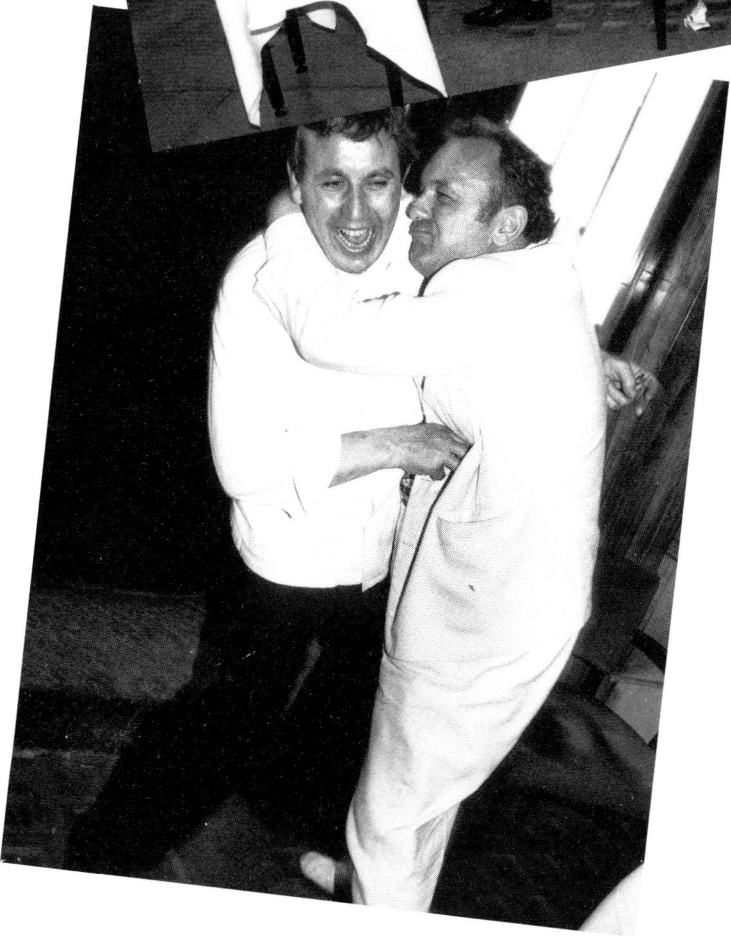

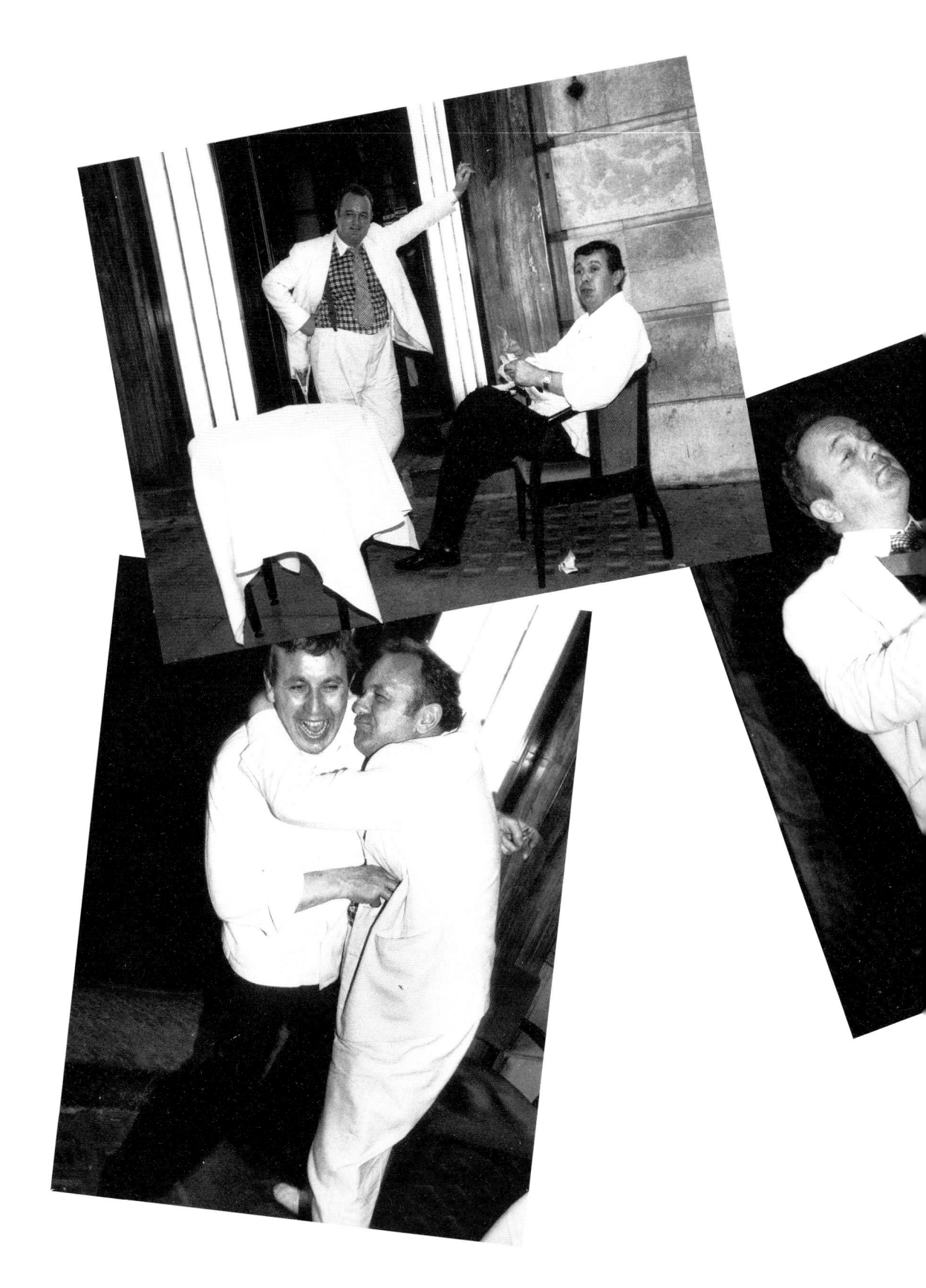

The celebrated occasion when, after an argument with Richard Shepherd, Peter closed the Brasserie before lunch, ate the appointments book and sat outside telling the clientele to go away. Shepherd remonstrated and, unknown to Peter, sent diners round to the side door. Press photographers provided an audience as Peter's mood moved from anger to exhibitionism.

in Albemarle Street) playing waiter, he revealed the splendours of much labour to Saturday-night wankers for whom he did not care a damn.

Just as Peter had wanted the pictures to look collected rather than bought, so he wanted the furniture in the restaurant to be old, comfortable and mature, as though it had all been there for ever – an almost impossible task for him, when Sunday was the only day on which he could scour junk and antique shops. I sent him down to Warminster to talk to Alexander Ballard, a tall, stooping antique dealer with the air of a dilapidated condor, who kept a ramshackle antique gallery in what had once been the local Conservative Club and Bowling Alley, and who had a remarkable nose for such a hunt; I, meanwhile, made the weekly trawl of London's scruffier auction rooms an absolute discipline. As is the way of such things, we bought far more chairs than were needed; some that had looked splendid in the seedy purlieus of Lots Road and back-street Marylebone looked little short of frightful when they reached Odin's, while others that had promised well enough when tatty and dishevelled were unacceptably vulgar when restored to velvet splendour, and had at once to be shed at the same auction rooms.

In cutlery, crockery and all the details of the restaurant, Peter wanted to apply what he had learned during the years in little Odin's. The taste and eye that had developed with experience were to be expressed even in the ashtrays and aprons; the latter were made by hand to his precise specification, tailored to reach the ankle of each waiter, no matter how tall or short, and then rejected because they hobbled the boys and prevented them from running up the stairs from the kitchen. His taste in cutlery was frustrated by cost and delivery delays. He designed plates that were larger than customary, with decorated borders, so that food need not be crowded and crammed but would seem elegantly composed and framed; one plate was made as a prototype, but the cost prevented him from pursuing the idea. Nothing went smoothly, and as he hated compromise, nothing was easy for those who helped him. He took great pains over the lighting, knowing, as usual, the effect that he wanted, but not knowing how to achieve it: he spent a fortune in Marylebone High Street with Mrs Crick, an antique dealer specialising in chandeliers and whimsical Victorian *coronae lucis*, whom he invariably addressed as 'Ma', but little that she sold him worked as he wished; he turned to the pasticheurs of the nether King's Road and fared no better; he was most successful with would-be antique pots and jars converted into lamps, for these conformed to his other wish, that the restaurant should be decorated with things that in some way made it look homely – his reason for hanging Imari dishes among the paintings, and putting an absurd *art nouveau* sculpture of an ivory maiden over the kitchen stairs.

All this frantic activity had barely begun when Peter and Susan decided to marry; on the Friday of the August Bank Holiday weekend in 1971, 27 August, they presented themselves, with Lionel Stirgess and me as witnesses, at the Marylebone Register Office, for a bleak ceremony that left us all feeling as though nothing sacramental had occurred. We also felt rather deceitful, for Peter wanted no one, and particularly neither Kirsten Benson nor Nicholas Vilag, to know of the marriage, and for months we had to dissemble. The wedding breakfast was lunch at the Connaught, where we toasted the bright hopes for the new Odin's. None of us would then have believed that the interventions of the local Medical Officer of Health, the GLC and licensing magistrates were time and again to delay its opening, that the lavatories would have to be moved downstairs after they had been installed and decorated upstairs, that a new kitchen floor laid in January 1972 would months later have to be dug up to accommodate new drains, that a ventilation shaft would have to be built to the full height of the flats above – and all this in a constant panic over the money that the first Odin's was always too small to generate.

The one benefit brought by the delay was that Peter continued to buy pictures for the restaurant. 'Buy' is perhaps too positive a word; he haggled (not a seemly thing to do with the patrician dealers of Bond Street), promised to pay within a few – unspecified – months and offered food as whole or part payment. In November 1972 I chanced to wander through Agnew's (which was once a stable-yard, and which many of us use as a short cut from Albemarle Street to Bond Street, maintaining a right of way) just as they were preparing an exhibition of twentieth-century British art, and saw Harold Gilman's magnificent *Negro Gardener*, an early work probably painted in the United States in 1905. The price was in the region of £1,500, but Julian Agnew, supposing that I was buying it for myself, reduced this to £1,200 or thereabouts, and I forced Peter to pay the bill promptly – though I half hoped that as he had never spent anything even approaching that sum for a picture, he might take fright and leave me with it. When Peter lent it to the Arts Council's Gilman retrospective exhibition at the Royal Academy in 1982, the author of the catalogue conjured the ghost of Velasquez as its inspiration;

art historians are occasionally over-enthusiastic, and I cannot share this hyperbolical view, but it suggests recognition of the portrait's astonishing quality in the control of a warm blonde tone, the even handling of its substantial paint, and the subtle use of the human figure as an object of still life yet at the same time suggesting a cool compassion for the gardener as a man.

The Gilman was consonant with Peter's loose policy of concentrating on modern British pictures, and was perhaps his most important – and certainly his most scholarly – purchase, challenged only by the vast Laura Knight; but he was not determined to be consistent, and when I suggested that he buy a large and slightly absurd picture by Richard Westall, a Royal Academy piece of 1831, because it matched the scale of the restaurant and was perfect for the west wall, he did not hesitate. As an early illustration to the first English translation of *Faust* (Lord Leveson Gower, 1823) it is of some small art historical interest, particularly so as Westall appears to have been aware of Delacroix's illustrations of the *Walpurgisnacht* episode issued in 1828. Not that such matters were of any concern to Peter; he merely enjoyed the pert nudity of the young witch Lilith, utterly hairless in armpit and delicately draped across the rima, as Faust assists her in the first steps of the frenzied dance in which all the other figures are already engaged. 'Did women shave in those days?' he asked me. I told him that I didn't know, but that in Delacroix's day I suspected not, since I had once seen a very bushy study of a nude by Ingres, his near-contemporary.

The Westall is a large picture, some eight feet tall, Faust and Lilith approaching life size, and the viewpoint demands that it hang low; Peter, courageously, decided to accept this, but his decision has resulted in frequent and occasionally extensive damage to the picture when guests have leaned against it or pushed the backs of chairs through it (it is now reinforced so that this can no longer happen). The carelessness of guests has been a constant hazard to the collection, and there have been startling examples of wanton damage: from Annie Swynnerton's large picture of a girl on a donkey a guest carved a section of canvas measuring some fifty square centimetres, and no small picture hung without glass near the quieter tables has proved safe from obscene graffiti or genital punctures.

The Fine Art Society (FAS) in Bond Street was for years the most prolific source of pictures for Peter. It was Alexander Ballard who introduced him to the gallery; Andrew McIntosh Patrick, its ebullient leading light, often dined at the first Odin's because he lived nearby, but had never let it be known that he was an art dealer (Anthony d'Offay also used the restaurant without attempting to sell pictures to Peter). AB, as Ballard is known, had long cared for Maxwell Armfield, an ageing painter whose roots lay in the tempera revival at the beginning of the century and all the belated Pre-Raphaelitism that that entailed; when Peter went to him for chairs, AB attempted to interest him in pictures. Max, then all but ninety, was still vigorously painting his reinterpretations of seventeenth-century Dutch still lives, and his mannered, esoteric, arcane and altogether tiresome astrological and mystical inventions. They had no appeal for Peter, but as they were much celebrated in Bond Street, he went, out of a politeness of sorts, to a party at the FAS in September 1971 that marked the opening of Armfield's ninetieth-birthday exhibition organised there by AB. Peter bought nothing, but he liked the atmosphere of the gallery, with its old-fashioned open fireplace and Victorian furniture, and took to dropping in whenever he viewed a sale at Sotheby's, across the road.

From his frequent visits developed a warm and trusting friendship with Andrew Patrick. On a Sunday evening in April 1973 Andrew invited him to a very private view of an extraordinary exhibition that was to open the following week, and Peter there and then made his first purchases from the FAS – two paintings by Gluck, the reclusive seventy-eight-year-old lesbian daughter of one of the founders of the Lyons tea-shop chain, who had not exhibited at the FAS since 1937. For *Bettina*, a cool and arrogant profile portrait of a woman in black, enlivened by an emerald ring, mannered fingers and an eyelid flushed with pink to match the mouth, only fifteen inches high, Peter paid the then astonishing sum of £1,270. It is a measure of his courage and judgement that he was not deterred by the thirty-five years of absolute obscurity in which Gluck's reputation had altogether evaporated, by the fact that her pictures were not supported by fashion or critical acclaim, nor by my misgivings that the market for her work might not last; he recognised strange new qualities of imagination, style and craftmanship, and did not hesitate.

The second Gluck, *Medallion*, was an austere double-profile portrait of the artist herself with her lover, Nesta Obermer, with whom, absurdly, she felt fused into one being. In the picture both women, their hair mannish and combed back to emphasise their noble profiles, face sternly into a hostile future with the high-flown determination that was commonly expressed as an ideal in the political art of the thirties. In its allegorical pretentiousness it is at least as absurd as much of the imagery employed by Gluck's contemporaries in Nazi Germany, though it represents nothing more serious than a 'marriage portrait' and the women's exchange of wedding rings on 25 May 1936; it hung in Gluck's studio as a challenge to all her visitors, and was known as *The You We Picture*.

In the financial crisis that almost destroyed Peter in the mid-seventies – precipitated by the machinations of a French wine merchant who had promised Peter exclusive rights to all the wine from some perfect little vineyard hidden away from the world, allied to the prolonged effects of the oil crisis that struck in the winter of 1973 and dragged on until 1978 – he was forced to sell both Glucks to the FAS, and it brought him close to tears. The measure of his long-term loss was established in November 1989 when *Medallion*, for which he had paid £880, was sold at Christie's for £58,000.

In August 1973 Peter bought another picture from the FAS – a stylish *Bacchanal* by Ernest Procter, typical of a pseudo-classical strand in English painting between the wars. The strong sexual element is camouflaged by exaggerated mannerisms as, urged on by a putto, a rushing pantomime of centaurs and white women surround a negress, their obvious intent made decorous and decorative. Many English painters of the period, Augustus John, Glyn Philpot and Epstein among them, were obsessed by the contrast of black and white female flesh, and by the possibility of contrasting lesbian enchantments – and Peter shared their lubricious curiosity.

In December 1973, when the art market was plummeting in response to the oil crisis, he bought yet more pictures from the FAS – charming, old-fashioned, intimate things by Lavery, Talmage, Gunn and Way, and even a rare and not particularly comely portrait by Tuke, who is better known for shafting boys' bottoms with sunlight than for painting faces. None of them was expensive, and it was almost the end of a spree. The last purchase of the year was at Christie's, when he bought a pair of beach scenes by John Noble, boldly painted, but no match for the quality of Gilman, Sickert and Knight. I sat with him through the auction and tried to deter him even when he was bidding, but failed, for he was convinced that whatever they cost, they were already paid for: during a flat patch in the sale I had made a telephone call and got a crossed line into a conversation between two crooked bookmakers exchanging information about a race that afternoon that would be won by a particular horse; I told Peter; without a word he left the saleroom, and when he returned he told me that I owed him a hundred quid, for he had put five hundred on the horse for himself and a hundred for me. I protested that I didn't want to blue that sort of money on a horse, but Christie's in the middle of a sale is no place for such argument and he hushed me with 'I'll take it out of your winnings.'

There were no winnings. The horse came second, but Peter had backed it to win, and not for a place. That crossed line proved very expensive, not only with the bets but with the paintings, for Peter would not relinquish the bidding and took it to the then absurd figure of £1,240. It was the first time that I saw him caught in the trap of vain competitive behaviour that is all too common in auction rooms, and that was to bedevil and embarrass him to the end of his days, but he was convinced that the horse would win and that his winnings from the bet would pay whatever he might be compelled to bid, and more.

Peter bought nothing more from the FAS until 1981. The long break in buying pictures that had begun with the oil crisis was extended by his ambitious conversion of the Coq d'Or into the Brasserie in 1976, but in 1981 he bought pictures by Brangwyn and Eurich, and by 1985 was buying pictures of museum standard again – in quantity, and for substantial prices. In May that year he bought two paintings by Frederick Cayley Robinson (which suggested a movement towards an esoteric taste that might at last accommodate the work of Maxwell Armfield) and a robust extravaganza by Brangwyn, *Marco Polo's Return to Venice*, that was a characteristic exercise in piling Pelion on Ossa. In July he bought a strong dark portrait of a Cornish fisherman by Christopher Wood, a melancholy picture that, in reflecting the painter's sombre mood in the late months of 1928, when other artists had fled the colony at St Ives and he was alone and found life there 'hard and bloody', also reflected Peter's occasional descents into depression when agencies over which he had no control frustrated him, and when alcohol diminished his intellectual ability to resolve such frustrations. Late in August he bought yet another Brangwyn, of jolly Spanish galleons, at £9,000 marginally the most expensive picture of a year in which he spent over £50,000 at the FAS alone. In 1987, writing on 'Collecting' in *Tatler*, Peter listed the purchase of another Gluck from the FAS in the previous year, and commented, 'There are many art dealers. I only use one, the Fine Art Society in Bond Street, opposite Sotheby's. They know their job...'

That article was intended as a child's guide to buying pictures, but it is robust in language and sentiment, and tells much of Peter himself. Wildenstein's, perhaps the largest, richest and most powerful dealers in the world (and art dealing at their level is the exercise of power), he describes as '...selling by names, often poor French paintings. You should go there if you wish to purchase famous signatures. It is very suitable for Americans.' He continues, 'The real collector loathes the kind of arse-hole who gloats over what a good investment he has made. He is the equivalent of the dentist who shows you the fine claret in his cellar and then gives you a bottle of rat piss with dinner. A picture should be bought because you love it, not for its potential increase in value.' This sound advice contains a barb: Peter's Harley Street dentist had indeed offended him with a meagre wine, and Peter made the comment on rat piss knowing that he read *Tatler* before putting it in his waiting room.

In the winter of 1975/6 Peter was itching with ambition to expand his business and to become the greatest restaurateur in the country. With the sale of the Glucks and other economies, the larger Odin's was recovering from the worst effects of the great wine débâcle; old Odin's – having failed as the fish restaurant in which Peter had wished to serve the best fish and chips in London – had been turned into a bistro that retained in some small measure the atmosphere of its first years (the upturned umbrellas in the ceiling had become its symbol) and offered a less expensive alternative to the new Odin's, and cash was beginning to flow easily for the first time in his life. He could well have bought more pictures, and would have been well advised to do so, for the art market was still deep in the slump from which it did not recover until Sotheby's flamboyant Mentmore sales in 1978 broke four years of gloom; but he did not. He chose instead to open the Brasserie.

His first idea was to take over the old Mayfaria Rooms in Quebec Street, just north of Marble Arch, which had been popular with

Patrick Procktor: Peter Langan, 1974. This is Patrick Procktor's cruellest portrait of Peter, painted when the oil crisis of 1973/4 had devastated the patronage and profits of the newly-opened second Odin's, and Peter had no money to spend on pictures and had even been compelled to sell his beloved Bentley.

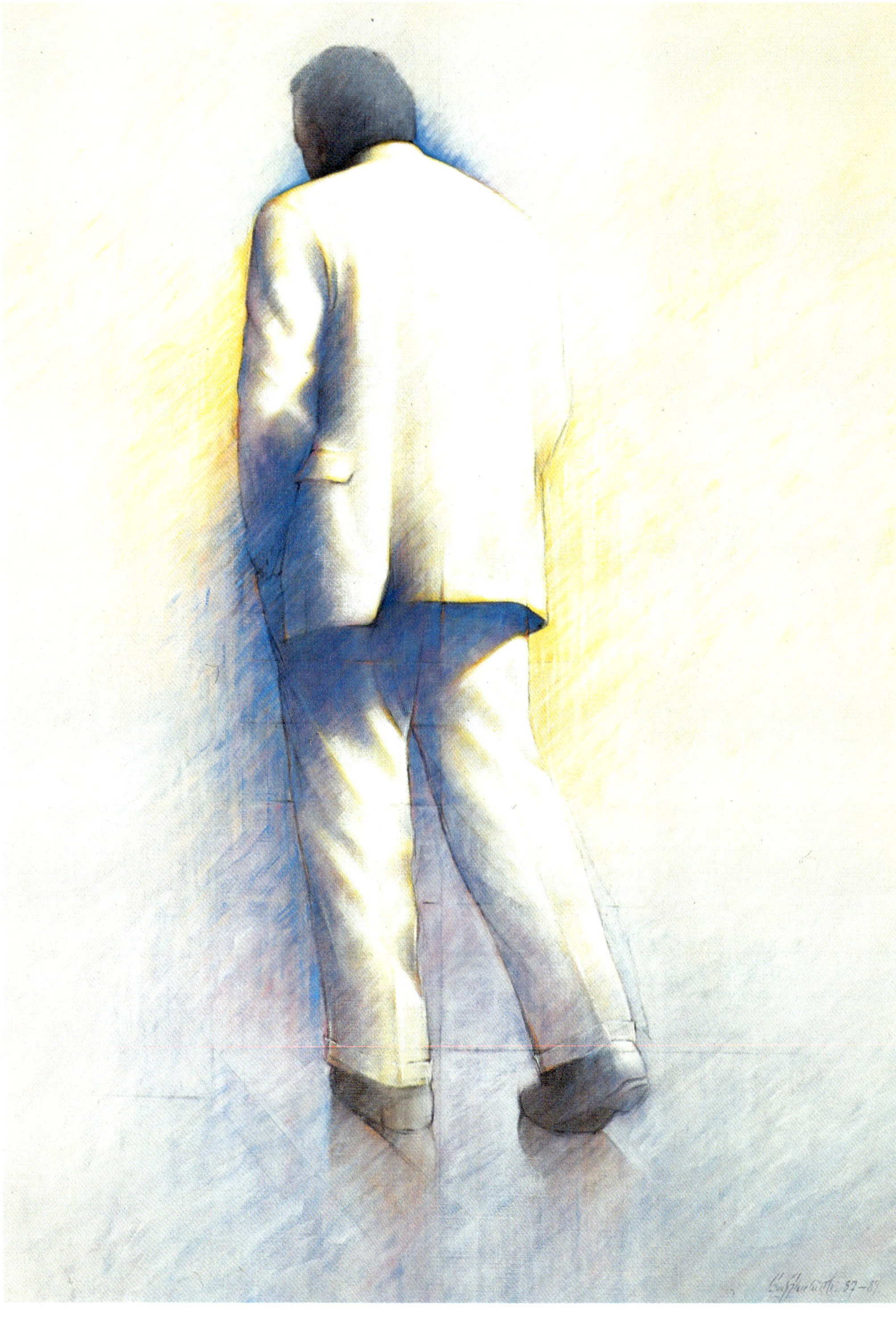

bourgeois flappers and their beaus between the wars, and had then become the haunt of spivs, GIs and girls on the game, to descend into a long, slow after-life as a supposedly sophisticated setting for the beanos of unsophisticated suburban Conservative Associations and organisations of that ilk. Peter's enthusiasm had to be restrained; the premises were not large, but were interesting enough, with the possibility of catering for private parties without disrupting the main restaurant, and upstairs there were small rooms that could serve as offices or, unofficially, as a flat that would allow him to 'sleep on the job', as he put it; I argued that it was in the wrong area, an unfashionable limbo tarnished by its proximity to Oxford Street and unlikely to attract serious trade by day or night, and that it might even be too close to Odin's, reminding him that the old Odin's had been very difficult to re-establish as an alternative to the new. He was obsessed by the idea of a flat above the business, as though some kind of sanity or salvation lay in his having a *boîte* of his own, and when, eventually, he turned against the Mayfaria, it was more because the lease was unfavourable than for any other reason.

Very soon after, on a bitter winter's day, he took me to the Empress Club in Berkeley Street, and suggested that he might take it over and run it as a brasserie. I could see from its general configuration that he still had in his mind's eye the brasserie in Brussels to which I had taken him years before, but I was appalled by the scale of the project. The room seemed huge and lofty – I had not seen it since I was a boy being treated by my stepfather, but time had not exaggerated my recollection of the marble vastness that encased those uncomfortable events – and that Peter, so recently in debt, so recently deprived of his favourite pictures and his Bentley, should propose the adoption of this great white elephant, hidden behind its canopied door, invisible to the passing public and known only to those who already knew it, occasioned alarm, dismay and dread, and the recognition of a megalomania that might, unfettered, lead to his destruction.

Within a week we were considering an alternative – the old Coq d'Or in Stratton Street. We sat there long after lunch, until it was empty of

Guy Gladwell: Farewell to Peter Langan. *Gladwell, another artist friend, spent some days with Peter in Blackpool on a wild goose chase for premises for a Brasserie of the North. It rained, Peter became deeply morose, and the project died. Gladwell spent his time drawing Peter's descent into alcohol, and later painted this picture of him in one of his many white suits, in characteristic mood.*

other patrons, and then wandered upstairs and down into the kitchens. The red velvet banquettes stank of stale grease and tobacco, and the kitchens of miscellaneous frightfulness, but the long room on the ground floor looked onto the street throughout its length, a vast west-facing window lit the back room, and the upper room seemed perfect for private parties, both intimate and grand. The kitchens were filthy, and crowded with old-fashioned contraptions dating back to the rebuilding of Stratton House in 1925 and the first restaurant there, better suited to the Science Museum or a train shed (before it became the stuffy and respectable Coq d'Or, the premises were known as the Blue Train Restaurant, described in 1930 as 'a fashionable rendezvous of London Society'), but the lavatories were impressive in their marble splendour and generous scale. Unlike the second Odin's, this was a working restaurant with a licence, and would not require time-wasting arguments with local authorities – no architects, no builders, no drains, no air vents; it needed nothing but the stamp of Langan's taste.

Immediately after the lease became his, we wandered round the restaurant again, with Peter behaving a little like Mole in *The Wind in the Willows* when he returned home; it was as though something distantly familiar had suddenly come close and proved neglected, worn and shabby instead of welcoming. Peter could shrug off such depressions – champagne helped – and he knew exactly the effect that he wished to achieve: he knew where he wanted to put shelves laden with cheap and battered books for people to steal; he knew where he would put pictures, though he had none to hang; he knew above all that he wanted nothing that resembled either the Coq d'Or or Odin's. He tore down a pair of handsome curtains and gave them to me – an act symbolic of the changes and the speed at which they were to be made.

I was not privy to the partnership arrangements with Michael Caine and Richard Shepherd. I know only that they were necessary, and that Peter thought Shepherd the best chef in London and a man whose ideas were so much in tune with his own that their working together would not be acrimonious. Peter wanted a brasserie that served breakfast at eight, omelettes at eleven, salami sandwiches at one, and toast and sticky pastries all afternoon, as well as proper lunch and proper dinner; he wanted sausages that came from Warsaw and Lisbon and all points between (he had a long passion for sausages, and believed that bangers and mash could be a great English dish if the sausages came from

Cumberland and the potatoes were fluffy and well peppered); he wanted national and international newspapers racked with wooden spines for all to read at will; he wanted everyone from Vienna to Madrid to recognise at once that his was a brasserie of the European kind, where no stranger would be repelled for wanting nothing more than coffee and the *Frankfurter Allgemeinschaft* when all around were munching their way through three full courses. I do not know why that dream died – only that it did so very quickly.

Peter had too little money to buy pictures for the Brasserie. I lent him a self-portrait by Henry Greaves, some oddments by Duncan Grant, and a few other modern British paintings that more or less conformed to the pattern of his own collecting, and he added two pictures by Guy Gladwell, a friend whose work had recently been exhibited at the Piccadilly Gallery. His only immediate purchase was of the huge view of St Paul's by Gerald Moira that hangs on the stairs. This I found in a sale at Bonham's, rolled with its painted surface on the inside of the roll (which explains the pattern of the cracks still to be seen in the picture's surface), and virtually invisible; like the Laura Knight at Odin's, it was the perfect size for its intended position – some twelve feet by eight – and opened the space in which it hung, with a crowd of figures under a colonnade and a wide view across a Thames busy with boats and cranes. It dates from 1910, and does not disgrace Peter's pictures by more famous hands.

Two coincidences about this painting please me. The first is that Moira was the painter of the great frieze that decorated the entrance of the Trocadero Restaurant, now forgotten and destroyed, but once a famous London haunt in which, as I recall from my very early years, they kept long-legged chairs for children – and it seems neatly proper that eighty years later a painting by Moira should decorate the one restaurant in London that could be described as the heyday Troc's present-day equivalent. The second coincidence is that Moira, though born in London, was of Portuguese parentage, and among Peter's last acts of patronage was the purchase of paintings by José Castro Maia, a young Portuguese painter working at the Royal College of Art on a Gulbenkian scholarship.

Though the main room of the Brasserie, opened in September 1976, was an immediate success – and still, more or less, conforms to the pattern that he laid down – Peter could not decide on the purpose or the atmosphere of the upper room. I spent some time with him, brooding, but could only suggest yet more pictures, and it was not until 1979 that he resolved the problem. He decided that as the work of Patrick Procktor had contributed so much to both the Odin's, perhaps Patrick should be asked to paint murals in the room, and he commissioned him to paint a decorative scheme based on wintry views of Venice, misty and mysterious. I suspect that I sowed the idea in his mind by showing him a small picture by Ippolito Caffi that had enchanted me with its subtly dimmed and foggy view from the Piazzetta, so alien from the conventional blue brightnesses of Canaletto and his imitators; or he may have caught the notion from another nineteenth-century Italian painting, a wintry landscape in northern Italy, a thing of ditches and pollarded willows, all soft pinks and greens subdued in the flat light, by Francesco Fanelli, bought some years before for Odin's (another of Peter's breakaway pictures, bought solely on his eye for quality, caring nothing for fame and reputation). Whatever the case, Patrick failed to conform to the idea of a February Venice, shrouded and glaucous, and produced a scheme that Peter damned as garish. Peter was abusive, threatened to whitewash the murals, and alternately raged and sulked; his final solution was to ask a carpenter from the Victoria and Albert Museum to conceal the mural on the south wall behind a battened panel, on which he could hang a miscellany of framed pictures, and to dull the others with several coats of tobacco-coloured varnish, which he claimed to have applied himself. Patrick's open views of Santa Maria della Salute and across the Giudecca, and his intimate glimpses of buildings on the Grand Canal and into backwaters – with odd references to the works of Canaletto and Carlevaris in his use of the Bucentauro and other details – are all obscured and muted by what apears to be the accretion of half a century of cigarette smoke. Princess Margaret was responsible for a minor damage when she attempted to scratch away the varnish with her fingernail and removed Patrick's paint as well.

More than a decade has passed since Peter's act of vandalism, and Patrick is still wounded by it; 'He certainly buggered it up' was his comment at the time of his winter exhibition at the Redfern Gallery in 1989, when his larger pictures were selling for £25,000 apiece. The south wall perhaps survives in perfect original condition under the panel, but as the Venetian views were painted direct onto the plaster they cannot be removed, and, sooner or later, all will be destroyed, whatever their state.

At the Brasserie Peter's circle of friends widened and he played clown to many a public and professional personality as he strove to become one of their number. Within six months of its opening, the *Sunday Telegraph* described the Brasserie as 'a casual, happy-go-lucky round-the-clock eating place ... crammed regularly with the new set ...' and Peter as 'host to the Seventies Swingers' – though of these the writer could name only Ronnie Corbett and David Hockney. He courted editors, actors and anyone who might pass for a celebrity of sorts, and became impatient with old friends who did not care to go with him into the bright lights. He engaged the constant interest of gossip columnists – so much so that his death was a matter for the writers of headlines and the readers of news on radio and television. When he challenged Michael Parkinson to a wager and it turned sour, he kept the issue running for months in his determination to extract every last word of publicity from it, long after those who might write the words had grown weary of the subject.

He drank champagne more readily than most ordinary men drink tea or coffee, and crippled his liver to the point at which a daily injection of some never-disclosed restorative drug became essential to his survival; soon after three every afternoon he grudgingly clambered into a taxi to Harley Street, 'off to that crooked quack for a jab of the elixir' ('crooked' and 'bent' were as much terms of affection as of abuse in Peter's vocabulary). He had not always drunk champagne: in the airless kitchens of the first Odin's he had taken to swigging Löwenbräu – the best, he claimed, of beers – and constant drinking had become to him what lighting cigarettes is to a smoker, a ritual of comforting gestures as much as a narcotic dependence; in the second Odin's, no longer condemned to life over hot stoves, he tended to drink Pouilly Fuissé; and it was only in the Brasserie, the noisy, fashionable and public place that he had conceived as a reincarnation of the Café Royal (but which was much more like the short-lived Blue Train Restaurant in its clientele and style), that he adopted the role of the rich Bohemian in a constant state of celebration. He always called it 'champagne', never 'shampers' or 'shampoo', and was touchingly puzzled when one of my older friends said that he'd be delighted to drink 'a glass of the widow'.

In 1981 he marked his fortieth birthday with a wake in the Brasserie, forecasting that it would be his last, so damaged was his liver. Such seventies swingers as John Osborne, Bobby Moore, Patrick Procktor and George Melly were at the long table; Melly, in red shirt and black fedora, raised his voice in song (though there were those who thought the sounds

Evening Standard *cartoon by Jak.*

"BE OFF WITH YOU CAINE, YOU'RE GIVING THE PLACE A BAD NAME!"

"LISTEN! IF MICHAEL CAINE HATED YOU *THAT* MUCH, WOULD HE HAVE ORGANISED A PETER LANGAN LOOKALIKE CONTEST?"

Sun *cartoon by Tom Johnston.*

more resembled an effort to blow bubbles between slices of ox liver) and touted his most recent record; playing his own link-man he described the Brasserie as a cat-house and Peter as its Madame. David Hockney was in America, but sent a print to represent him; Philippa Toomey of *The Times* brought a large bunch of wrinkled silver balloons that clung to the ceiling like a minor work of Andy Warhol when Peter released the string.

Seized by the idea of opening a brasserie in America, Peter paid many visits to Los Angeles, each time asserting that he might not return – he enjoyed as many final performances as Maria Callas, and in rather better voice. In January 1984 he held what he claimed was positively his final farewell party at the Brasserie, but few old friends were there, for by then his life had become entirely a performance for gossip columnists and the editors for whom he wrote book reviews, epistles on the art of cooking and revelations of his daily life. In shirt-sleeves, he wore for the occasion bright red braces and white trousers as crumpled with sleep as was his face, but he behaved with muted decorum and did not get drunk; it was indeed a dull evening, for without real friends with whom to joust he could not raise his spirits. William Hickey and his *paparazzi* went away disappointed.

He reappeared in London from time to time to issue news bulletins and renew his wardrobe of the white suits that had become his uniform. Though they had the shape and style of a flour sack, these were made for him and were very expensive. Whenever Peter returned from Los Angeles, a young tailor came to the Brasserie, measured and remeasured the increasing girth in front of as many patrons as might be drinking in the back room, and a few days later delivered three identical suits. Peter wore them night and day, slept and sweated in them, dumped them in washing machines and donned them damp and crumpled, and when they yellowed, as inevitably they did, he simply threw them away. If any survive, they deserve a place in the costume collections of the London Museum and the V & A.

His tales of Los Angeles varied little over the seven or eight years that it took to establish his restaurant there. He repeatedly asked me to go with him, but I refused. In London I could get up and walk away from him, but in America, where he spent a fortune on whores, lawyers and champagne, and was cheated by those in whom he was compelled to put his trust, mugged by drug-crazed blacks who threatened him with AIDS-infected needles as well as revolvers, and generally victimised by

American society, walking away, even when he became intolerable, would have been unforgivable in a friend. The restaurant had the character of a mirage – always there, but never achieved; most men would have relinquished the project, but Peter was driven by a demon and would not. At last, in the summer of 1987, he was sure that it would be brought into being and was once again in London in search of pictures.

In the *Tatler* article, written at that time, Peter's first rule for buying pictures well is 'It is advisable not to view a sale after a heavy luncheon and essential not to purchase when you are plastered. I speak with the voice of experience.' He did indeed, for he had just broken that rule at Sotheby's. He gave me lunch in a Korean restaurant in Lancashire Court, off Bond Street, tasting a dozen expensive dishes and then passing them to me to finish – our long-established pattern of behaviour on such occasions – and then we crossed the road to Sotheby's to see the picture that was his reason for picking my brains. He had told me nothing of it, other than that he wanted my opinion.

Porters hauled the picture into view, a portrait of a man, lacking a frame. 'Oh that's only a bit of a picture,' I exclaimed. 'It's the upper half of something that was once full length, cut down to a conventional long half-length in size, but the composition doesn't fit – you can see that for yourself. It's north Italian – Brescia, Bergamo – somewhere in that region – 1530ish. Damaged by water – it has ruined the left side and may well have rotted the bottom half, which would explain the cutting down. And the dark background is nothing but a massive repaint – hideously disruptive. Why are you interested?'

'What's it worth?' asked Peter.

'Needs cleaning, relining, restoration. If it is to look convincing you also need a good period frame, or a fake that will pass for one. Altogether it might take £5,000 to make presentable – and even then you'll only have half a picture by a minor painter who will never be securely identified. I suppose, if pushed, you might buy it for £5,000 and spend another £5,000 tarting it up, but there must be better things for that sort of money across the road at the Fine Art Society.'

'Are you sure?'

'Yes.'

'Christ almighty. I've just spent forty thousand fucking quid on that, and you tell me it's only half a picture. I was drunk.'

He had not then paid for it, but only had it knocked down to him. I suggested several stratagems for getting out of the deal, among them taking a loss by paying Sotheby's their two commissions, but, Irishman to Irishman, Grey Gowrie, Sotheby's chairman, resisted Peter's charm and he had to pay. I last saw the wretched fragment a few weeks before its dispatch to America, slightly tarted up by a jobbing restorer, and in a hideously unsuitable frame of rough-planed timber that had been crudely gilded; it looked like a varnished reproduction masquerading as an oil painting.

This rash purchase disposed of more than half the sum set aside for pictures to be bought for the Los Angeles restuarant, and was the cause of Peter's diverting his patronage from the trade and directing it to the work of young untried painters. He had a peculiar skill in hanging, and could make witty and perceptive use of pictures that others could see only as aggressively dissimilar. I knew that he had some pretty rum things in hand, oleographs and primitives, for he and Susan had come to me for advice on how to frame them (as well as to inspect two dogs I had lately rescued), and that he had always intended to mix the mature and valuable with the mature and worthless no matter how much money he had to spend, but mixing old junk with raw new paintings was a severe test, even of Peter's rare ability.

One of the young painters who caught his eye was José Castro Maia, the Portuguese boy about to enter the Royal College on his Gulbenkian grant, from whom he bought a large allegory of London based on a Horse Guardsman, a black taxi, and an Egyptian figure in the British Museum. From Lucy Erskine, who had just left the Byam Shaw School, he bought several still lives and a rich, warm study of a nude. From Martin Mooney, who left the Slade School in 1985, he bought more still lives – rich, tenebrous, mathematically organised compositions that harked back to Spanish paintings of the seventeenth century.

It was, however, the work of Alexandra Haynes, just at the end of her second year at Cheltenham School of Art, that most excited him. He recognised in her bold colour and the streaking character of her brushwork a landscape painter of such assurance as might relish the challenge of decorating a restaurant, and he not only bought from her almost all the work available, but at once commissioned her to go to Los Angeles and paint a series of Californian landscapes for the restaurant there, delivering her to the care of David Hockney. This was decided in the Brasserie one late August morning, when all the furniture in the back room was cleared so that Alexandra could unroll canvas after canvas, most of them eight feet tall, with Peter growing more enthusiastic by the minute, saying 'I'll have it,' or 'Paint something over that tree,' or 'Put something yellow in the foreground,' or 'Change the colour of the lake,' or even 'Cut a couple of feet off the bottom and eighteen inches from the side and you've got a good picture [he had learned something from his £40,000 Sotheby portrait],' while the champagne flowed, for Alexandra, a bright young thing, could match him glass for glass.

Peter was also attracted by some fresh little pictures of nudes, people and domestic episodes – very much in the tradition of the New English Art Club, the colour bright, the palette clean, the painting assured, and the imagination moribund – by Sandra Fisher, wife of his old friend Ron Kitaj, and he bought at least one from her modest exhibition in Cork Street. More than any, he wanted one in which a young and comely naked man was actively engaged in copulation, but objected to the prominence of his large red scrotum, low and full between the thighs. Out on the pavement, still gazing at it through the gallery window, he said, 'I'd have bought that fuck picture if he hadn't got such swollen balls. She ought to paint them out. Do your balls hang behind your legs when you're on the job? I'm sure mine don't. I'm sure mine get tighter. She's not much good at cocks, either.'

In the winter of 1987, when Peter had accumulated in his house in Essex all the pictures that were to be sent to Los Angeles, he asked me to write a valuation list that could be used for Customs formalities. It was agreed that we would take the train to Colchester the following Saturday morning, and that I should meet him at the Brasserie at nine-thirty. The Brasserie was not only closed, but could have been a house of the dead; after ten minutes of thumping on the doors and rapping on windows, a sleepy Spaniard came to the side door and asked my business. I told him that I was meeting Peter.

'He no here.'

'Where is he?'

'He was here. He gone.'

'Gone where?'

'I don't know. To get breakfast. Perhaps round the corner' – this accompanied by a gesture towards the Ritz.

I tried the Ritz – not the easiest thing to do when, to a degree bordering on morbid obsession, all that concerned the waiters was the

David Hockney: Peter Langan, 1972. *This portrait is perhaps the first drawn by Hockney specifically as a menu cover for Odin's. It shows Peter seated on the banquette just inside the window of the original restaurant, looking down its narrow depth, with the upturned umbrellas that masked the ugly ceiling just indicated above him.*

absence of a tie from about my neck and none would listen to my enquiry. Returning to the Brasserie I was compelled to repeat the pantomime of thumps and raps until the Spaniard let me in to wait. I waited for an hour, and then went home and rang Susan, who was on the point of driving to Colchester to meet us.

Half an hour later, Peter telephoned.

'Where are you? We were supposed to meet.'

'I'm here. At home. I came to the Brasserie but you were not there.'

'Why didn't you wait?'

'I did. For more than an hour. I even tried the Ritz.'

'Why the Ritz?'

'Your Spanish waiter said you'd gone there for breakfast.'

'Bugger breakfast. I was with a whore in Shepherd Market.'

'At half-past nine in the morning?' Whoring at that hour seemed to me almost as immoral as watching television in the morning.

'I slept on the floor of the Brasserie and woke up ready for a wet mouth – and this woman's really good and friendly.'

It was my turn to swear, and I did. I was used to Peter's broken invitations to lunch – the disconsolate loneliness of peanuts and orange juice in the back room of the Brasserie, waiting for a friend who neither appeared nor sent a message; I was used to his invitations to dinner and had learned the wisdom of snacking before setting out to meet him, for far too often what were intended to be quiet and private evenings became rowdy accretions of guest after guest as Billy Connolly, Joan Collins, Donald Sutherland, Pamela Stephenson and ill-assorted celebrated nobodies arrived to take up their tables but be seduced to his – and as the circle grew, so the prospect of dinner at a reasonable hour diminished and, unnoticed, I would slip empty away. All this I could accept, knowing the importance that such people had assumed in his life, knowing how useful they could be to him and how little use I could be if the lenses of the *paparazzi* were to flutter for his benefit; but that I could be ditched on a cold December morning simply because Peter had wakened with an erection and wished to stick it in a wet mouth round the corner really cut me down to size. It hurt. I did not see him for several months, most of which he divided between Los Angeles and the restaurant that he was nurturing in Coggeshall, near his home in Essex.

He left Susan to see the dispatch of the pictures, and for her sake I made the Customs lists. It was a miserable business, for the extravagant purchase of the Italian portrait had compelled him to pad the consignment with what could only be described as back-street auction-room rubbish, and framed posters. In his *Tatler* article he had written, 'Reproduction today is of such a high standard that it rivals numbered lithographs. If cash is short, posters framed as pictures, cutting out everything except the image itself, are ideal. Under glass they look like "originals".' They do not, and such a statement from the man who had paid for the printing of Patrick Procktor's *Pea Soup*, and who knew full well the importance of a wide variety of print techniques to David Hockney, was preposterous. I doubt if he really believed it, but he may have been trying to convince himself that what he proposed for Los Angeles would look well enough when hung. I had seen such an exercise in the so-called Langan's Bar and Grill, a franchise restaurant in Down Street, Mayfair, in which Peter had been involved in 1985, where cropped posters had been embellished with scribbled signatures and such dedicatory inscriptions as 'For Peter, with love from Juan Miro' – Peter only laughed and said 'The cunts will never know' when I pointed out that Miro was a Catalan and used the form *Joan* for *Juan*; 'If it was signed *Joan*,' he said, 'they'd think it was by Miro's wife.' In spite of their expensive and often sympathetic frames, these posters seemed to me to be nothing but a worthless and distasteful deception of a public that would blindly hold them in awe as originals simply because Peter had a reputation as a famous collector and a friend of Hockney. 'Ghastly pictures,' said one of his friends, 'but there was no money and his partners didn't understand.'

I saw Peter several times in the summer of 1988. He seemed quieter, more controlled, and even sad without the driving demon of the Los Angeles restaurant – a post-coital condition perhaps; he even kept appointments and never once was drunk. He was trying to lose weight, ate little, and eschewed champagne in favour of low-alcohol beer, but the gestural tippling continued at its customary rate. His spirit was not tranquil. He talked of re-hanging the pictures at Odin's, but I think it was no more than casting about for something to do. We went to galleries and auction houses, but he could find nothing that pleased or excited him, and his general response was 'Jesus! the prices!'

I went to Turkey for most of September, and he telephoned almost every day to see if I was back. On Friday 30 September we had lunch at the Brasserie, peacefully and soberly; he seemed obsessed by AIDS, not for himself, but for the loss of many friends; only his proposed autobiography occupied his energies, and he complained of the effort it cost him – 'Everyone will want the gossip, but I want to write a *serious* book.' Three weeks later, on 21 October 1988, I saw the headline of the *Evening Standard:* 'ROWING LANGAN IN A BLAZE'. On 8 December 1988, he died.

Peter was recently described as 'perpetually inebriated, occasionally droll, usually boorish – a charismatic bully whose genuflectory activities gave a new meaning to "*le patron mange ici*"'*. He was indeed drunk far too often and for far too long; barrack-room vulgar, or shrewd and waspish, he could be very funny; his boorish bullying of friends and waiters was embarrassing, distasteful and sadistic, for his victims could not easily escape; and he was maniacal in his concerns for cunnilingus and fellatio, gloating with speculation, his anticipatory enjoyment almost as fulfilling as the act. But this vignette is less than half the true portrait, and omits all that was warm and generous, intellectual and spiritual. 'Intellectual' and 'spiritual' are perhaps rare adjectives for Peter, but I am convinced that his response to pictures was both, and that in an age when a good eye mattered more than a pinprick doctorate in art history, he could have been a brilliant museum director, and even today would have served well as a trustee of such a gallery as the Tate.

In spite of that conviction, it is Peter the performer, the clown and the darling of the gossips who is uppermost even in my mind. As we walked back to Odin's after lunch at the White Tower one warm October day, he bought a whole box of green figs – largely to demonstrate the profit margin in the prices charged by a respected restaurant, though I do not think he was unaware of the female sexual symbolism of the ripe bursting flesh. We ate a few, and then Peter offered one to a passing woman: 'Have a fig, my dear,' making 'fig' sound quite indecent. He enjoyed her dismayed refusal, and asked the same question of almost every woman we met on our way; all behaved as though he had said 'fuck' and not 'fig', all refused, and one made such a fuss about it that a patrolling policeman crossed the road and sent us briskly on our way.

On Christmas Eve 1972, Peter came to dinner. I had just moved into my present house, and though he had been to it several times during the

---

*Kay Daventry, 'Eating out in the Eighties', *Tatler*, December 1989, p. 177.

long-drawn miseries of gazumping, and had indeed convinced me that I should continue to raise my bids, it was his first visit as a guest and I fussed in his honour, stuffing a boned partridge into a duck, the duck into a chicken, the chicken into a goose, and the goose into a turkey that Peter himself had sent me. I hoped that he would recognise his bird, but be surprised by what it contained; I anticipated a gasp as I flourished a carving knife and with a single slice through the centre revealed the contrasting rings of flesh that might resemble an exotic chunk of marble. Other guests arrived, but Peter did not. No one answered his telephone. An hour later than planned we went down to the dining room without him – and then the bell rang. It was, of course, Peter; he had called a cab to his flat in Osnaburgh Street, told the driver that he could not remember the address but would recognise the house, and fallen into a deep sleep. On entering the road the driver had tried to wake him, but could not, and had been resourceful enough to take him back to Osnaburgh Street and wake him there – only to be cursed for his common sense and commanded to return to Kensington. Having told this tale over the first course, Peter turned to his neighbour, the American widow of an interestingly disreputable Irish art dealer, and observing that she had done her painterly best to prettify features that resembled both Bette Davies and a Cavalier King Charles spaniel, asked, 'And what beat are you walking later tonight?'

In the early winter of 1983 we spent a boozy evening in a St James's bar run by Beth Coventry, Peter talking dirty with Lucien Freud and lusting after a young woman with a blonde moustache who had strayed in from the street. We were supposed to be dining at the Ritz and trying their Beaujolais Nouveau, but Peter was distracted by the girl, who had brazenly engaged him in a French kiss and let his pudgy hand wander up her skirt; I had the impression that she was using Peter to elicit a response from Freud, and when she refused his invitation to come with us to the Ritz, was convinced of it. Beth seemed vaguely put out by the performance and disappeared into the kitchen; I volunteered to go home and thus relieve Peter of any obligation to please me when he might much prefer to be pleasuring his loins; Peter then asked the girl in the plainest terms if she would spend the night with him; she refused, and we left her alone with Freud and walked round the corner to the Ritz. I remember nothing of that dinner other than that Peter talked endlessly of 'cunt' and grew soggy on the meagre Beaujolais. At midnight, thinking of dogs that must be walked, I left, but he followed me into the arcade and shouted insults at my back. His customary valediction was 'Take it easy.'

Peter was an atheist, and believed nothing taught him in his Catholic boyhood; for him there was no atonement, no purgatory, no salvation, no immortality. *Carpe diem*. There must be, nevertheless, in recollections prompted by small events and happenings, an immortality of sorts in the minds of those who loved him.

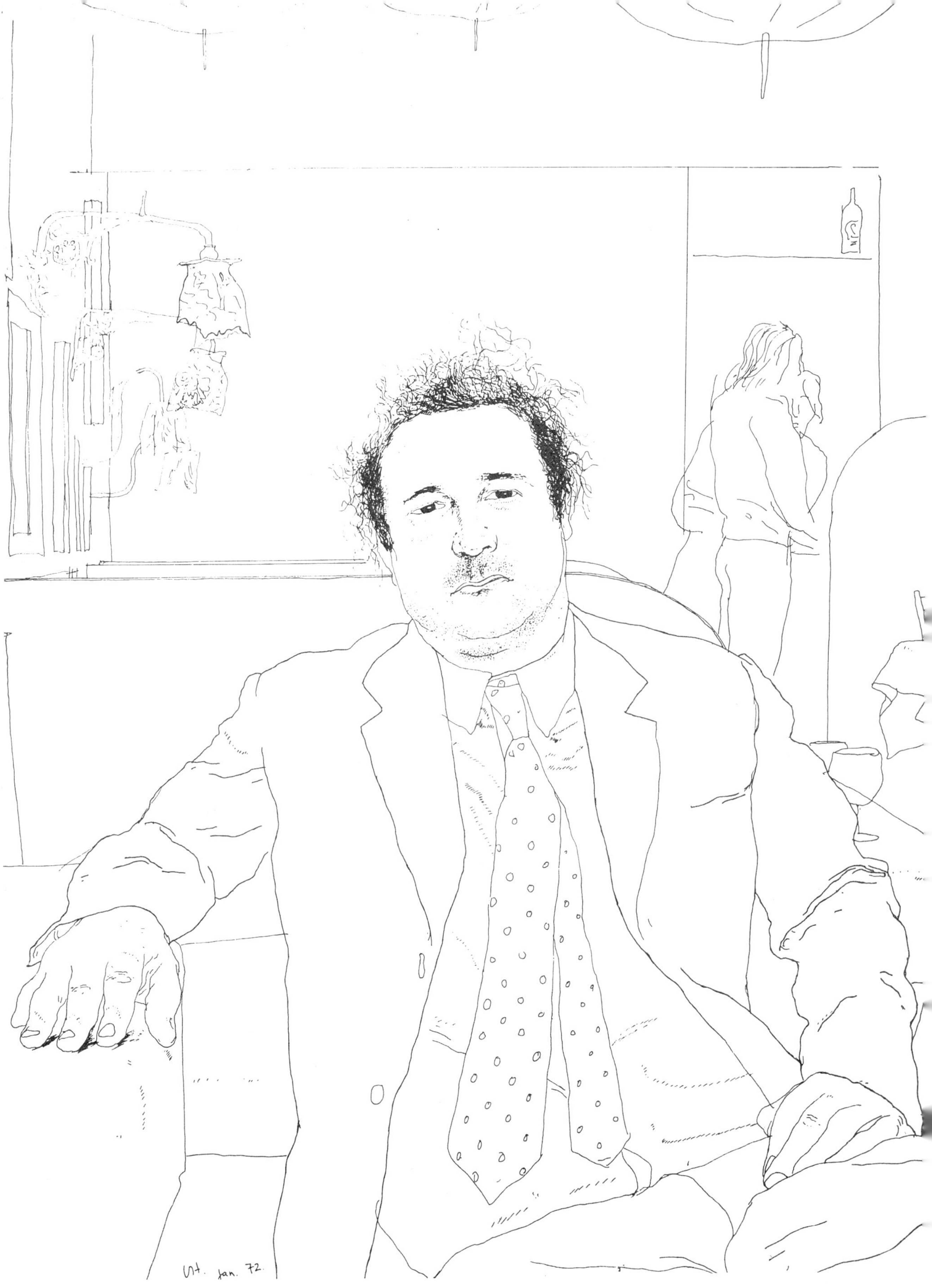

Ut. Jan. 72.